The ArtScroll Series®

Rabbi Nosson Scherman / Rabbi Meir Zlotowitz

General Editors

The Informed

Published by
Mesorah Publications, ltd

Soul

Introductory Encounters with Jewish Thought

by Rabbi Dovid Gottlieb

FIRST EDITION
First Impression . . . November 1990

Published and Distributed by
MESORAH PUBLICATIONS, Ltd.
Brooklyn, New York 11232

Distributed in Israel by
MESORAH MAFITZIM / J. GROSSMAN
Rechov Harav Uziel 117
Jerusalem, Israel

Distributed in Europe by
J. LEHMANN HEBREW BOOKSELLERS
20 Cambridge Terrace
Gateshead, Tyne and Wear
England NE8 1RP

Distributed in Australia & New Zealand by
GOLD'S BOOK & GIFT CO.
36 William Street
Balaclava 3183, Vic., Australia

Distributed in South Africa by
KOLLEL BOOKSHOP
22 Muller Street
Yeoville 2198
Johannesburg, South Africa

ISBN:
0-89906-570-8 (hard cover)
0-89906-571-6 (paperback)

Typography by CompuScribe at ArtScroll Studios, Ltd.
4401 Second Avenue / Brooklyn, N.Y. 11232 / (718) 921-9000

Printed in the United States of America by Noble Book Press Corp.
Bound by Sefercraft Quality Bookbinders, Ltd., Brooklyn, N.Y.

This ספר *is dedicated*
in loving memory of
our father, grandfather
and great-grandfather

Nathan Millar o.b.m.
נחמיה ב״ר ר׳ גדליה מילר

נפטר י״ג שבט תש״ח

השקיע בדור זכה בדורות

Dovid & Lieba (Millar) Gottlieb
נחמיה, רחל, חוה, אביגיל גוטליב
ירמיהו, מרים (גוטליב), יוסף דושינסקי
מרדכי נח ודבורה (גוטליב) אידלשטיין
פינחס גוטליב
חיה ביילא גוטליב
אלעזר מנחם מנדל גוטליב

Menachem & Gail (Millar) Fishbein
חיה אסתר
שושנה שיינדל
אברהם צבי נחמיה
אביבה מרגלית

הרב לוי יצחק הלוי הורוויץ
בן הרה"צ ר' פינחס דוד זצוק"ל — דער באסטאנער רבי

GRAND RABBI LEVI I. HOROWITZ

CONGREGATION BETH PINCHAS

1710 BEACON STREET
BROOKLINE 46, MASS.
REGENT 4-8100

ב"ה

The greatness of Torah is in incorporating תורה שבכתב, the written law, and תורה שבעל פה, the oral law. Each provides special opportunities.

In the oral message, one benefits from the human touch, from voice expression and from physical mannerisms, as the ear listens to the spoken word.

Written communication, on the other hand, affords the possibilities of focusing in on a subject with greater concentration, אינו דומה שונה פרקו מאה פעמים לשונה פרקו מאה פעמים ואחד, "One who repeats his chapter a hundred times is not to be compared with one who repeats it a hundred and one times" (Hagigah 9b). Even the spoken word is best understood when one can see it. Thus, the Torah was given not only verbally, but also in visible form, as it is stated in the Torah, "and the entire nation *saw* the voices."

My special talmid, Rabbi Dovid Gottlieb has, until how, provided the oral lessons of Torah for many years in a most unique way, giving thousands the chance to literally experience the רואים in a visual demonstration of Sinai. He has thereby influenced the many with whom he came in contact to become close to Hashem.

I classify this book as his תורה שבכתב, written word. The book provides a wonderful opportunity for people to concentrate on the message he has beautifully delivered for so many years. I am certain that this written word will influence many more Jews who, until now, were not fortunate enough to hear his oral message.

May the Ribono Shel Olom grant him continued hatzlachah in his ongoing endeavors to provide means of kiruv to the distant ones and to give renewed strength to those already committed.

המצפה לישועת השם ולהרמת קרן ישראל

Over a Half Century of Torah Commitment and Service to the Jewish Community

MT. WILSON LANE • BALTIMORE, MARYLAND 21208 • (301) 484-7200

November 1, 1990
13 Cheshvan 5751

Harav Dovid Gottlieb allowed me to study the manuscript of his work, "The Informed Soul." It is an impressive accomplishment, indeed.

He has brought the power of an incisive mind and skills of an analytical thinker to bear on elucidating the depths of a number of issues in Judaism. The results are a clear and stimulating discussion that provides meaningful insights for those involved in investigating the treasures of Judaism.

I heartily recommend this work to all who are seeking to better understand the heritage of the Jew.

Sincerely,

Rabbi Yaakov S. Weinberg
Rosh HaYeshiva

(718) 436-1133

RABBI YAAKOV PERLOW
1569 - 47TH STREET
BROOKLYN, N.Y. 11219

יעקב פרלוב
ביהמ"ד עדת יעקב טאוואמינסק
ברוקלין, נ.י.

בס"ד

יום א' ט' מרחשון תנש"א

חזיתי לידידי הרב היקר והנעלה מו"ה דוד גוטליב שיחי'

הנודע בשערים בארץ ובגולה כהוגה דעות ומאלף תושי'
בין שכבות אחינו הדורשים ומבקשים נתיבות האמונה ומסילות התשובה,
שהעלה על הכתב לקחו ושיעורו שדלה מבארות התורה ומבועי החכמה.
וכבר איתמחי גברא בהשפעתו המוצלחת לעשות נפשות לאבינו שבשמים
ולהדריכם במושכלות של אמת ומסורת היהדות. ויהי השם עמו לראות את
חיבורו עושה פרי לתועלת הרבים ויזכה עוד רבים בשנים להרביץ תורה
ואמונת אומן כיד השם הטובה עליו. כעתירת ידידו ומכבדו

יעקב פערלאוו

❧ Contents

Section I:
Foundation

The Truth about Religion	17
Cross-Cultural Critique	37

Section II:
Understanding

Mysticism, Meaning and Mitzvah	57
Rights, Freedom and Tolerance	83
The Chosen People	107
Providence and Suffering	127

Section III:
Appreciation and Application

Prayer, Petition and Merit	159
Teshuvah —	
Return and Reconstruction	177
Afterword —	
Impulses to Teshuvah	197

⤚§ Foreword

The chapters of this book are organized as lectures together with questions and answers on both beginning and advanced levels. Outlines are provided at the beginning of each lecture. Part of the reason for this format is the fact that the material originated in lectures delivered at Yeshivat Ohr Somayach and Neve Yerushalayim in Jerusalem and to audiences in the United States, Canada, the United Kingdom and the Republic of South Africa. The questions are also selected from these encounters. But even more central is my hope that the reader will feel *personally addressed* and will participate in the ongoing search for self-discovery and truth. Although each question in this book is given an answer, it wasn't always that way. Some of the questions took years to answer! Each one advanced our shared understanding and clarity. Now I eagerly anticipate many new collaborators.

Many of the problems addressed in the lecture discussions are among the most fundamental in both Jewish and general philosophy. The problem of evil, the efficacy of prayer, repentance, the nature and limits of rights and equality, the relationship of truth to religion — each of these has a long history and could easily fill a whole volume. I have no illusions that these problems are now settled! Nevertheless, I hope that some progress has been made, especially in approaching them from the perspective of traditional Judaism.

It is my responsibility and my pleasure to acknowledge the people who aided my efforts in this project. My brother Professor Roger Gottlieb, Rabbi Nota Schiller, Elya Meyer Klugman, Jonathan Rosenblum, Professors Yehuda Gellman, David

Widerker and Jonathan Ostroff read parts of the manuscript and offered many valuable suggestions, as did Mrs. Judi Dick, the reader for ArtScroll. Rabbi Sheah Brander offered valuable editorial advice. Years of learning with Rabbi Beryl Gershenfeld have greatly benefited my grasp of many of the topics in this book. My students and critical audiences have stimulated innumerable improvements over the years. An anonymous donor provided me with the support to devote a year to writing. Rabbi Eli Teitelbaum arranged that support and has advanced the process from its inception. Finally, the office staff at Ohr Somayach endured patchwork manuscripts and hurried deadlines over a period of a year and a half, producing uniformly excellent work. My thanks especially to Helena Emmett, Rosalie Moriah and Deena Yudkofsky. I only pray that they feel the results justify their efforts.

To Rabbis Nosson Scherman and Meir Zlotowitz is due a special debt of gratitude for their encouragement and support. I consider it a privilege to participate in the ArtScroll Series of English Torah publications. Thanks are also due to Shmuel Blitz of ArtScroll Yerushalayim, for his constant attention and care.

My parents, Alfred and Sylvia Gottlieb, and parents-in-law, Mordechai and Chana Martin, have encouraged and supported all my personal education endeavors. Their help and inspiration is invaluable. Whatever I have been able to accomplish, the major portion of credit is due to my wife Linda whose encouragement and steadfast belief made it happen. שלי ושלכם שלה. Finally, my heartfelt thanks to my Rebbe, the Bostoner Rebbe, Rabbi Levi Yitzchak Horowitz Shlita, who has been my inspiration, posek, guide, advisor and friend for the past twenty-nine years. גדול המעשה יותר מן העושה.

Rabbi Dovid Gottlieb
Jerusalem
Tishrei 5751

The
Informed
Soul

Section I

Foundation

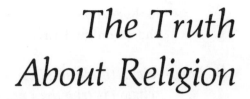

The Truth
About Religion

I. *Two criteria for religious decision*
   A. Usefulness — religion is a resource for individual and social goals — different religions for different cultures/individuals — eclectic
   B. Truth — religion describes (part of) reality and how to live appropriately in relation to it — religion chosen on the basis of truth

II. *Pragmatic attitude implies no religion is true: if some religion is true then pragmatic choice is irrational and irresponsible.*

III. *Religions are pairwise incompatible, therefore at most one is wholly true.*
   A. Catholicism — man is a god
   B. Islam — Mohammed is prophet
   C. Judaism — vs. (A) and (B)
   D. Hinduism and Buddhism — vs. Creation at finite past time

IV. *"Common core" to all religions — no positive religious content*

V. *How to investigate the truth of religions — theology must have unique empirical consequences which are true.*
   A. Excludes religions which have no empirical consequences
   B. Excludes religions whose empirical consequences can be explained independently for their religions' tenets — conquest and expansion, quality of personal experience

    C. Excludes religions whose empirical consequences are false

VI. *Judaism is the oldest extant religion with no false and some true (Deut. 28) consequences — start investigation there.*

ৎৢ The Truth about Religion

OUR TIME IS ONE OF UNPRECEDENTED FREE-
dom, and unprecedented confusion, concerning religion. Liberal democratic societies allow an almost
unlimited variety of religious expression. General
education and the mass media place before the individual dozens
of competing religious philosophies and life-styles. As a result,
each of us is faced with a choice which is at once both momentous
and excruciatingly difficult. *Momentous* — religious commitment
profoundly affects our values, world-view, activities, indeed all
aspects of our lives. *Difficult* — in the midst of so many
alternatives, expressed in different languages, ensconced in
different cultures, scattered across the globe, on what basis is one

to decide? We shall consider two criteria for decision: *usefulness* and *truth*. After describing the criteria and choosing one as appropriate for the initial investigation of religion, we shall develop the general framework for that investigation and note Judaism's unique position in it.

The criterion of usefulness evaluates religion in terms of the antecedently given goals and values which it serves. These goals and values may be individual, promoting sensitivity, "spirituality," personal focus and the like. Or they may be social, contributing to stability and cooperation. In general, they have little to do with truth. One may feel more sensitive and "spiritual" reciting an ancient Greek prayer or performing a Hindu ritual without believing that these religions are true. Pharaoh's belief that he was a god was useful to ancient Egyptian society (and to him personally!) despite its falsehood. A person employing the criterion of usefulness — the *pragmatist* — may be expected to make free use of the full range of humanity's religious history and present, and in an eclectic manner. There is no reason for him to be bound to a single tradition or philosophy. Mass in a great cathedral appeals at one time, the fasting-feasting of Ramadan at another, and the Jewish Sabbath at still another. The pragmatic individual (or society) may choose a mix of religious elements (including his own new inventions) most useful to his needs. This mix will change as conditions and needs change. The religions of ancient Egypt, ancient Rome and contemporary Los Angeles will certainly differ widely, as well may the religion of the twenty-year-old from his own religious expression at age seventy. Finally, the criterion of usefulness includes the possibility that no religion at all will be relevant to the needs of the individual or society and hence religion will be entirely rejected.

In contrast to usefulness, the criterion of truth evaluates religion for its accuracy as a description of the real world. Most religions contain assertions concerning certain aspects of the world. These usually include: the origin of the universe and its end, the nature of man and his future, the most fundamental forces which govern nature and human history, and certain particular historical events such as prophecy or miracles. A person employing the criterion of truth — the *realist* — will be concerned only that these descriptions be true. If he finds a religion whose descriptions are true, he will commit himself to it. Any religion whose descriptions are false he will reject. Furthermore, unlike the pragmatist, the realist expects ultimate religious agreement and consistency if a true religion be found. For, whatever is true is so for everyone, in any society or culture, and in all ages.

Both of these criteria are widely employed today. Many believe their chosen religions to be true and are passionately committed to converting the rest of the world. Many others view religious expression as a private choice, determined by the individual values.

Are these approaches equally valid? Is there any reason to think one more appropriate than the other? We can say at least this: *As long as it is possible that some religion is true, the criterion of truth must be employed. The pragmatic approach is relevant only if the possibility of truth has been rationally ruled out. It is irrational to make religious commitment depend upon immediate personal or social usefulness when these may conflict with truth.* In order to see that this is so, we should distinguish two possibilities: (1) believing the religion, and (2) adopting religious practices without believing it. Both are irrational as long as the question of truth has not been settled.

Consider (1): A religion may describe God or gods, the soul, the origin of the universe, etc. Imagine using personal growth and satisfaction, or social stability and cooperation, to decide to *believe* those descriptions are *true*. It is like believing there is oil under your back yard because you enjoy fantasizing being rich, or believing the chest X-rays mistaken because you want to continue smoking. The criterion of usefulness leads to belief for reasons which give no evidence of truth, and that is irrational. Now consider (2): It may seem that if the religion is not believed but only practiced, no more irrationality can be involved. But this is a mistake, since practicing one religion precludes believing *another one*. It is clearly folly to invest in Christian practices if you believe Islam to be true. So even deciding religious practice on grounds of usefulness has an impact on belief — a negative impact — bymaking belief in some other religion impossible. And again that decision — to not believe other religions — is being made on grounds irrelevant to truth. It is like not believing the prediction of an eclipse tomorrow because it will mess up my horoscope. The criterion of usefulness leads to disbelief for reasons unrelated to truth, and that is irrational.

To summarize: If there is no truth to be found in religion, then of course the pragmatic-eclectic approach is appropriate; religion becomes an aspect of self-expression, on a par with art, music, etc. But until we are *rationally convinced* that all religions are false, it is unjustified to adopt a pragmatic stance *by default*. First must come an investigation of the possibility that some religion is true.

In order to apply the criterion of truth to religion, two preliminary observations are in order. First, religions contradict one another, therefore *no more than one religion can be wholly true*. This will be clear if we consider some examples. Many Christian groups assert that a certain man was God. Islam flatly denies that any man was God, and asserts in its turn that Mohammed was a prophet, which Christianity denies. They cannot both be right. Now Judaism denies both their assertions so at most one of the three can be wholly true. All three agree that the universe was created by a deliberate Divine act and has existed for only a finite time. Hinduism and Buddhism disagree with this assertion.[1] For any pair of religions there is some proposition concerning which they disagree. This means that as realists, we cannot be content

---

1. Smith, Huston, *The Religions of Man*, Mentor Books, 1960, pp. 81, 103-4.

with the variety of world religions. All but one (perhaps) are false (at least in part) and hence unworthy of belief and commitment. We cannot accept the laissez-faire attitude: "Christianity for the Christians, Islam for the Moslems, etc." We would not rejoice at a variety of contradictory beliefs in medicine, engineering or geography. Similarly, contradictory beliefs in religion mean that the vast majority of people make their most fundamental decisions based upon false assumptions. As realists, we must be prepared to reject religious falsehood in order to find religious truth.

Second, it is sometimes suggested that there is a core of common belief and value to the major world religions. This core includes a commitment to morality and spirituality and a sense of the integration of the universe. Religions differ chiefly over matter of style and ritual. Perhaps all religions are *partly* true — the core is true, and the rest is really optional for a realist. This suggestion has the virtue of reinforcing our laissez-faire tolerance of other religions: Each accepts the same core truths and expresses them in its own individual style. But it cannot stand up to scrutiny. Recall the contradictions mentioned in the last paragraph. What shall the core contain? It cannot have an account of creation, since religions differ on that subject. Nor do they agree concerning who have been prophets or which scriptures are genuine. Their views on the soul, afterlife, the nature of God, the end of history, etc. vary widely. None of these matters can be included in the *common* core. What then is left? Perhaps morality? But morality itself is not necessarily religious at all: A mere commitment to some actions being right or good, and others wrong or evil, without conception of God, creation, the soul, etc. can hardly be called religion. Thus the "common core" idea fails and we must finally abandon our uncritical tolerance. If a true religion is found, the rest will be false and indefensible.

How can it be determined if a religion is true? Since we are talking about true descriptions of matters of fact, discovery of this truth is not different in principle from the discovery of any other truth. Ordinarily, truth is investigated using the "scientific method." Therefore it seems that the truth of religion should be investigated in the same way.

Some oppose applying the scientific method to religion on the ground that science and religion address very different realms in different ways. They claim that science seeks to understand the physical world, while religion addresses ultimate values and other "spiritual" matters. But this is a half-truth. Religion is concerned with values and spiritual matters, but it also commits itself concerning matters of fact. Consider, for example: (1) The universe came into existence *ex nihilo* at some time in the past. (2) Man is not a physical-chemical-electrical machine. These are assertions of Judaism which are open in principle to scientific investigation. Indeed, it was almost universally accepted in the nineteenth century that (1) had been scientifically refuted, whereas the advent of the "Big Bang Theory" has restored considerable interest in (1). The opinion of most current brain researchers is against (2), although any conclusion is premature and there is some interesting evidence in support of (2).[2] Clearly, (1) and (2) are assertions concerning facts and thus the appropriate province of science. Insofar as religion purports to truly describe the objective world it is in principle open to scientific verification.

Application of the scientific method to religion requires care. To test any theory, it must predict something we can directly observe. If it makes no such prediction then it cannot be tested at all, and so has no claim on our belief. Thus a theory of leprechauns too fast to be seen or caught, too light on their feet to be heard or weighed, etc., is a theory for which in principle we can have no

---

2. Hooper, Judith and Teresi, Dick, *The 3-Pound Universe*, Laurel Books, 1986; Penfield, Wilder, *The Mystery of the Mind*, Princeton U. Press, 1975; Popper, Karl and Eccles, John, *The Self and Its Brain*, Springer-Verlag, 1977; Puccetti, Roland and Dykes, Robert, "Sensory Cortex and the Mind-Brain Problem," *The Behavioral and Brain Sciences* 3:337, 1987; Sabom, Michael, *Recollections of Death: A Medical Investigation*, Harper and Row, 1982.

evidence. Such a theory we can have no reason to think true, hence it can have no claim on the belief of a realist who is searching for truth. A religion which contents itself with recommending certain practices as "noble" or "ideal," and which describes only matters which can never be tested or observed in any way, is out of the running.

A second group of religions with no claim to truth are those which lack *unique* predictions. That is to say, what they predict could be agreed to by other competing points of view. Even if such predictions come true, they do not support the credibility of that religion vis-a-vis the relevant alternatives. Because this point is often missed, with tragic consequences, it bears elaboration.

As a first example, consider the fire-walkers.[3] They cross burning coals barefoot without injury, and take this as evidence that they are protected by a saint of their religion. Some years ago a group of atheists attended one of their demonstrations. More than thirty of the atheists also walked the coals and almost all escaped injury. The explanation seems to be that the foot is insulated by the response of natural skin oils to super-heating. This immediately deprives the religious walkers' experience of any force as evidence for their beliefs since we have an alternative explanation for their experience. Their prediction is thus not unique to their religion.

Similarly, those religions which use rapid expansion and/or conquest as evidence of truth are guilty of ignoring alternative explanations. First of all, they have each other to contend with. If Islam can boast hundreds of millions of the world's population among its adherents, so can Christianity. And both must contend with the obvious secular explanation that conversion by the sword is bound to be effective. Imagine a Jew being taken into exile to Babylonia. His Babylonian guard taunts him: "I guess you

---

3. *Science Digest*.

stubborn people will finally have to recognize our gods. After all, we won the war! You can see for yourself that our gods are very powerful." How could a Jew withstand this "empirical" argument? He may reply: "Our prophets have been predicting this conquest for a century. It is *our* God who has punished us by enabling you to win the war." As long as there is an alternative Jewish explanation for the events, they cannot verify the competing religion over Judaism. This point applies equally to the Christian interpretations of the last two thousand years of exile. Their claim that it was punishment for not accepting their messiah is convincing only if one is ignorant of the Jewish explanation of punishment for our failures. (Of course, their claim is also troubled by the return of Israel and Jerusalem to Jewish control without any massive conversion of Jews to Christianity taking place.)

The tragic consequences of failing to demand unique predictions come when people are invited to test the truth of a religion via their own experience. The devotee will tell them: "We believe in god so-and-so who runs the world, transmigration of souls, etc., etc. We don't ask you to accept this on faith, or to believe a prophet, like other religions. Test it yourself! Our religion predicts that if you join the ashram, sit cross-legged, eat mushrooms and say 'Om' for thirty days, you will have unique feelings and experiences. All it takes is one month for you to verify our religious teaching in your own experience!"

The unsuspecting religious explorer thinks to himself: "Why not? Nothing taken on faith, a direct test in my own experience — what could be a better test than that?" So he sits cross-legged and eats his mushrooms, and lo and behold in thirty days *he has the predicted experiences!* Doesn't that prove the devotee's claims? The devotee thus wins a new convert.

The fallacy in this procedure should by now be apparent. The prediction of having those experiences upon sitting cross-legged etc. for thirty days is not *unique* to the religion which believes in god so-and-so who runs the world, transmigration of souls, etc. etc. It is open to an atheist — or for that matter a Jew or anyone else — to say: "We reject your belief in god so-and-so and your other strictly religious beliefs. However we are prepared to acknowledge your mastery of a certain area of practical psychology which predicts that sitting cross-legged etc. for thirty days produces certain experiences. Since we have no reason to reject your purely psychological predictions, their verification provides no evidence that your religion is probably any more true than our beliefs."

We have seen thus far that for a religion to be of interest to a realist, it must meet two conditions. (1) It must make testable predictions. (2) The predictions must be unique to that religion. The first excludes Confucianism and Taoism, which make no testable predictions at all.[4] The second excludes Hinduism and Buddhism which make only experimental predictions, and the popularity arguments of Christianity and Islam.[5] A third obvious condition is that the predictions come true; this excludes those branches of Christianity which predict Jewish exile until Jews accept the Christian messiah. What then is left?

Judaism is left. Judaism has made unique testable predictions which have come true. Consider the following excerpts from Deuteronomy, chap. 28:

> It will come to pass if you do not listen to the voice of the Lord your God to guard to do all His commandments and statutes which I command you this day...God will cause you to be smitten by your enemies... and you will be a horror to all the kingdoms of the earth...your ox shall be slaughtered before your eyes and you shall not eat from it; your ass shall be taken by force and will not be returned to

4. Smith, *op. cit.*, chaps. 4,5.

5. *Ibid.*, chaps. 2,3.

you; your sheep shall be given to your enemies and no one will save you; your sons and daughters shall be given to another people and your eyes shall see and languish for them all day long and you shall be powerless; the fruit of your soil and all your labor shall be eaten by a nation which you do not know. . . God will bring you and your king. . .to a nation which neither you nor your fathers have known. . .sons and daughters shall you have, but they will not be yours, for they shall go into captivity. . . God will bring a nation against you from afar, from the end of the earth, as the eagle hovers, a nation whose speech you do not understand, a nation of fierce countenance who knows no consideration for the aged and shows no favor to the young. . .he will besiege you in all your gates and high and fortified walls in which you trust. . . and you will eat the fruit of your own body, the flesh of your sons and daughters. . .in the siege and distress with which your enemy distresses you. . .And God will scatter you among all the nations from one end of the earth to the other. . . and under those nations you will find no ease and there will be no resting place for the sole of your foot. . .And God will return you to Egypt in ships. . . and you will be sold there as slaves and maidservants. . .[6]

This prediction is remarkable in its description of details which *could not have been anticipated* and which easily *could have been unfulfilled by events.* If (a) the conquering nation had been a neighbor, or (b) had not been a world power (coming from "the end of the earth"), or (c) had spoken a language known to the Jews (e.g. Greek), or (d) had not slaughtered civilians indiscriminately, or (e) had not engaged in protracted siege, or (f) had left the conquered population on the land, or (g) had taken them in one group into exile (as did the Babylonians), or (h) we had not

---

6. The reference to return to Egypt follows Targum Onkelos and Yonasan, and not Rashi and Ibn Ezra.

migrated all over the world but remained, (e.g., in the Northern Hemisphere) or not reached the Americas, or (i) we had found some other place to settle independently (recall Herzl's suggestions of Uganda and Argentina), or (j) we had not been returned to Egypt in ships for sale as slaves,[7] *then the prediction would not have come true.* Here we have ten independent conditions, each quite improbable. Often nations are conquered by their neighbors who are local powers with a known language; not always are civilians slaughtered or is protracted siege necessary; exile is a rare consequence of conquest (the Romans especially took care to preserve the native population and economy, the better to collect taxes), and a world-wide scattering is almost unique in history; return to Egypt in boats of excess slaves could not have been anticipated; and that world-wide exile lasting twenty centuries should provide no other haven is not naturally expected. The probability of *all ten* conditions coming true is the *product* of their individual probabilities. So that even if we thought the probability of each condition was 0.5, (which is clearly too high) the probability of all ten occurring is 0.0009765, i.e., 1 in 1,000. If we set the probability of each condition as 0.25, (again probably too high) the probability of all ten is 0.0000009, i.e., 1 in 1,000,000.

Thus we have a clear, testable prediction from a Jewish text. Is it *unique*? How would other religions and philosophies have regarded this prediction? They would have no reason to believe it or accord it any credibility: From their perspective, there is no Jewish God who cares about treatment of orphans and widows, Sabbath observance, animal sacrifices and the rest. They would evaluate the prediction on the basis of probability, and hence rate it as one shot in a thousand, or a million. That is, they would reject it as not credible. *Thus it is a unique, testable prediction.* The fact that it has come true counts as straightforward evidence that Judaism is true.

---

7. Schurer, E., *A History of the Jewish People*, Edinburgh, 1890, p.11.

Of course, one true prediction does not suffice to confirm an entire theory. Nevertheless, as realists we should be encouraged. Here is a religion which dares to risk public verification and has to its credit at least one very remarkable success. So far, we have no excuse to retreat to usefulness in deciding our religious orientation. The investigation must continue, and Judaism must be its starting point.

Questions & Answers

LEVEL ONE

Your stress on eliminating what you call false religions sounds very intolerant to me. Are you suggesting we go back to the middle ages and burn heretics at the stake?

No, nothing I said would take us that far. I merely pointed out that when people disagree about matters of fact we don't rejoice over the disagreement. Rather, we look for some way to settle it — some way to discover who is right. What you call "elimination" of false religions should ideally be the result of investigation and education. However, there is a real problem of dealing with people who hold what we judge to be false beliefs concerning matters of public importance. People who smoke in public places, or run stop signs, or sell marijuana, and who sincerely believe they are not endangering others, are not tolerated in our society. Where to draw the line on these matters is a difficult issue.

I don't understand how you can talk about a scientific proof of religion. Even when it describes what you call the "objective world," it talks about things like the soul, Olam Haba (the world to come), a non-physical God who created the universe. Surely science cannot prove these things!

Well, with respect to the soul, the sources cited in footnote 2 claim to have scientific evidence of the soul in action; you are invited to look them over. A non-physical Creator might be inferred from the fact of creation (as described in the "Big Bang Theory") and the occurrence of miracles. It is true that there is scant scientific evidence for *Olam Haba*,[8] but this belief can be indirectly supported by the evidence for the rest of the system. In science also we cannot test everything a theory says. If the parts we test are confirmed, we extend credibility to the whole theory.

If I were that Babylonian soldier, I wouldn't accept the answer that the Jewish God is punishing the Jews. That is much too ad hoc and self-serving. It is much more reasonable to attribute my success to my gods.

You may be right. Remember, I only asked how the Jew could withstand the argument, not how to convince the Babylonian! But remember that the Jew's answer was not made up on the spot. The prediction was on record for many years. That can hardly be called *ad hoc*.

You point out that the probability of the prediction in Deut. 28 is very low; so low that no one else would have agreed with it, and no one else can explain why it came true. How do you explain it?

Well of course we believe in prophecy, so there is no problem. But for those who don't. . .

You ended by saying that the investigation must continue. How do you envision the rest of the investigation?

---

8. Some evidence can be gleaned from the account in Samuel I, 28: 11 ff of Saul's conversation with Samuel after the latter's death, and from dreams recorded in the Talmud and Midrash.

First, we need a survey of the rest of the predictions in the Bible which are precise enough to be tested.[9] Second, we need to examine Jewish survival: *to define* what survives and evaluate possible explanations. Third, accounts of miracles must be verified. Fourth, the impact of Judaism on world civilization must be assessed and possible explanations evaluated. From all of these there will be enough evidence to rationally justify the belief that Judaism is true.

If you do that, what happens to faith? Doesn't faith mean believing precisely when you do not have proof?

If so, did the prophets have faith — they who directly heard God speak? Or those who saw open miracles like the generation of the Exodus? Jews were never asked to believe something irrational, to make a blind leap of faith. They were asked to be *faithful*, to act consistently and courageously on the basis of what they knew. That is the real test of faith.

But didn't our ancestors express blind faith when they said, "We will do and we will hear?" They committed themselves to the Torah before they even knew what it was!

I can agree that their commitment was unique in being absolute, unconditional and unlimited. But I would not call it *blind* — not after witnessing the plagues in

9. Some predictions are couched in poetical language difficult to understand precisely. In addition, we must choose predictions for which we have *independent evidence that they were made before the events predicted.* For example, the predictions in Lev. 26:14-46 refer to the Babylonian exile (see Ramban on Lev. 26:16). But as long as a critic could assert that they were written after that exile, they are no proof that the Torah contains true predictions.

Egypt, the crossing of the sea, the pillars of cloud and fire leading them in the wilderness, the manna, etc. Their own experience taught them their God is powerful, intelligent, knowing and has a special relationship to them. Responding to *their* knowledge with such a commitment is hardly *blind* faith. It is rather a form of *trust*, no different in principle from trusting one's doctor (though different of course in *degree*). What traditional Judaism requires is our *faithfulness* to God as an expression of our trust in Him, and this is eminently reasonable.

৵ Questions

LEVEL TWO

I don't understand your distinction between the two criteria, usefulness and truth. Surely usefulness includes truth. How useful can it be in the long run to believe something false?

Your reference to the long run is half the answer. In the short run, false beliefs can certainly be useful, as in the case of Pharaoh's divinity, or in the case of Constantine's use of Christianity to unite the Roman Empire. And then it has been argued that certain false beliefs may be useful even forever. Plato suggested such a "noble lie" in the Republic (that people are born with different quality souls which determine their social roles) to insure social stability and cooperation. You are right that in certain cases usefulness requires truth, but in many cases it does not. In the latter cases the criteria are distinct.

Cross-Cultural Critique

I. Impossible to understand and evaluate action/practice/ institution without background of acts, beliefs, values.

A. Facts — physical (surgery), legal (dictatorship vs. democratic emergency powers)

B. Beliefs — human sacrifice for communal good (compare lifeboats)

C. Values — breeding for beauty/brains; censorship to protect ruler/security

II. Examples of Torah background

A. Facts — mikveh — for men and High Priest, not for cleanliness; Yom Kippur as self-flagellation or spiritual focus; Talmud as final authority

B. Beliefs — Oral Torah as absolute — tradition from Sinai; victimless crimes.

C. Values — complete Torah control of life, compare opera, sports, war; self-development vs. society's needs

❧ Cross-Cultural Critique

LET US IMAGINE THAT WE ARE PROFESSIONAL anthropologists. We are placed in a new, different and in some ways alien culture as temporary observers. Our goal is to attain some understanding of that culture. We will observe the natives' actions, examine their artifacts, attempt to understand their language and converse with them concerning various aspects of their lives. Furthermore, since we are human beings observing other humans (and not robots or some non-human living species), we cannot remain permanently detached from our observations. At some point we will also evaluate what we see, both generally and personally. Generally: is it right or good that people should live this way? Personally: can we learn anything for our lives from the way these people live? Now, in order for understanding to be achieved and evaluation to be valid, we must obey the Great Axiom of Anthropology:

> AN ACTION, PRACTICE OR INSTITUTION CAN BE UNDERSTOOD ONLY IN TERMS OF THE RELEVANT BACKGROUND OF FACTS, BELIEFS AND VALUES OF ITS HOME CULTURE.

First we shall look at a few general applications of the Great Axiom in order to appreciate its fundamental role in interpreting what we observe. Then we will see its effect upon certain aspects of classical Judaism.

Imagine an aborigine visiting a surgical operating theater. What does he see? Someone is wheeled in, stuck with needles, gassed, cut with knives, sewn with needle and thread. . .! To him this looks like a diabolical torture chamber. (Perhaps this is what they do to political dissidents?) We know that the patient is ill and that this is the best way we possess to help him. The difference between torture and surgery lies in *the factual background of what we observe.*

A man is walking peacefully down the street. A police car appears and the man is immediately handcuffed and taken away. Is this arbitrary use of force? Again, perhaps. But not if a curfew has been declared publicly and this man violated it. *Understanding what we see depends upon legal facts as well as physical ones.*

These two cases illustrate the necessity of filling in the complete background of physical and legal facts for our observations even in circumstances with which we are familiar. This is all the more important when we are observing a different culture.

We turn now to the background of beliefs. In ancient times (and up to a thousand years ago in South America) various societies practiced human sacrifice. Didn't they understand the value of human life? Perhaps they were prey to periods of psychological disequilibrium in which they became totally irrational and irresponsible? No, this is to completely misunderstand at least some of them. They believed that without human sacrifice the whole community would suffer. The gods will withhold rain, for example. Many will die of thirst and hunger. *In their minds* they faced an excruciating moral dilemma: whether or not to sacrifice an individual for the overwhelming good of many others. Men have faced the same dilemma in modern times in the famous lifeboat cases: should a few individuals be cast overboard in order to save the rest? *Given their belief,* we understand their practice in an entirely different light. Needless to say we will evaluate them — their mentality, values, etc. — very differently. Instead of appearing as primitive savages enormously removed from our perspective, they appear almost modern. (The "almost" registers their mistaken belief that rain depends upon human sacrifice. Given that belief we see that their values might very well be identical to ours.) This case illustrates the necessity of seeing the action "through the eyes of the agent." We need to know his beliefs about what he was doing in order to understand what it meant to him. Only then can we evaluate it relevantly.

Finally, we come to the last element of background: the values which the observed actions or practices are designed to serve. Imagine you observe a man and woman who want to have children. They apply at a government office, undergo certain tests, and are denied permission. You ask for the criterion by which such decisions are made and are told: "We rate the applicants' physical beauty and estimate the probability of their offspring being sufficiently beautiful. A certain minimum score is needed for permission to be granted." Horrible, isn't it? The right to have a family shouldn't depend upon esthetics. But suppose instead the explanation is this: "We rate the applicants' intelligence and estimate the probability of their offspring being severely mentally retarded. If the probability is too high, we deny the application." Somewhat less horrible perhaps? After all, the severely mentally retarded are usually wards of the state, and often suffer considerably. Perhaps bringing such children into the world is irresponsible? Or suppose it is the high probability of physical malformation that is the criterion? Whether the practice of the society represents a gross violation of human rights or the response to a difficult moral dilemma depends upon *the values which the practice serves.*

The same point is illustrated by censorship. Every society practices censorship, if only to protect its security. Some governments use this practice to protect their power. Between these two extremes are many debatable cases. Some years ago a screenplay depicting an airplane hijacking was aired on national television. The following week there were three airplane hijackings. Interviewed at the end of the week, the author said that if he had imagined his work would contribute to air piracy he would never have released it. Perhaps it should have been censored? In any case, one cannot understand the significance of a society's practice of censorship until it is clear *what value that practice is designed to protect.*

These cases illustrate the necessity of understanding the values of those whose actions we observe. This is part of "seeing it through his eyes" and understanding its meaning to him.

When we consider the institutions and practices of classical Judaism, the need to scrupulously apply the Great Axiom is especially great. There is so much ignorance and misinformation concerning the factual background, beliefs and values of classical Judaism that the danger of misunderstanding is enormous. We will now consider seven cases of widespread misunderstanding due to failure to apply the Great Axiom to aspects of Jewish living.

(1) In some people's minds, the use of a mikveh (a "ritual bath") is associated specifically with women, menstruation, sexual relations and cleanliness. Theories of the significance of taboos, sexual inferiority and other imaginings have then been concocted to explain the significance of this practice. But the associations

upon which these theories are based are inconsistent with the *legal facts*. The Torah in its *totality* prescribes mikveh for *men and women*. When the Temple was standing, men went to mikveh as frequently as women, and even today there are large groups of men who visit the mikveh *daily*. Although menstruation does necessitate mikveh, so do a host of other conditions: giving birth, contact with a corpse, seminal emission, contact with certain types of dead animals, etc. Although under certain conditions, immersion in a mikveh is required in order to permit sexual relations, such immersion is also required for many other activities: entry into the Temple, eating of consecrated foods, physical contact with a Kohen, etc. On Yom Kippur, the service of the High Priest required that he immerse himself in a mikveh *five times!* (How "dirty" or "inferior" could he have been?) Finally, absolute cleanliness of the body is a *precondition* for immersion in the mikveh: the mikveh cannot be used as an instrument to produce cleanliness. From this discussion it should be clear that unless the entire legal definition of the institution is taken into account, it will be completely misunderstood. As a result the theories proposed to explain it will have no connection with the Jewish reality.

(2) A novice anthropologist thrust into Yom Kippur as his first Jewish experience might view it as self-flagellation (fasting for twenty-five hours, standing with no shoes, crying). This view founders on the fact that the average observant Jew feels little or no hunger or thirst on Yom Kippur! How can this be? Think of experiences which are very absorbing — listening to a rock concert, reading a novel, watching the last quarter of the Super Bowl for example. Don't we often forget our hunger or thirst at those times? The tap on the shoulder which will turn you around at the bus stop will not even be felt in the middle of a concert. (There is even a physiological basis for this. For a nerve to fire, a certain threshold of stimulation must be crossed. When we are absorbed in a certain experience, the thresholds of nerves in neural pathways which are not related to the present experience are

higher than normal.) For the (physically healthy) observant Jew, Yom Kippur is just such an experience. He is so absorbed into the Jewish meaning of the day — introspection and self-evaluation, intimate dialogue with God, expiation of sin and cleansing of the personality — that normal bodily sensations cannot intrude into his experience. The anthropologist's view of Yom Kippur is thus *inconsistent with the psychological facts.*

(3) Classical Judaism accords the Talmud absolute authority. Any decision arrived at by the Talmud is absolutely binding. Some interpret this fact as evidence that traditional Jews are naturally servile and obedient; they accept whatever they are told without question or critique; everything established in previous generations is beyond criticism; creativity and originality of thought are of no value. This interpretation is falsified by the following fact: Aside from the Bible, *no other book enjoys the status of the Talmud.* The Mishnah, Maimonides' Code, the Shulchan Aruch, and all other works of interpretation and codification were subject to later critique, and none was accepted in all its details. (This is not to imply that anyone, at any time, may freely choose to accept or reject what he or she pleases from these works. There are legal rules and scholarly standards for valid critique, but none of those works has absolute binding authority.) *This historical fact invalidates the proposed interpretation.*

These three cases illustrate the care that must be taken to assess the full factual background, including facts of all kinds — legal, historical, psychological, economic, etc. Failure to do so results in complete misunderstanding of what has been observed. Next we examine the background of relevant beliefs.

(4) The Jewish tradition can be divided into the written (the Bible) and the oral (all the rest). Traditional Jews regard it all as binding. Some interpret this along the lines of case #3: Since only the written Bible is the word of God and all the rest is man's interpretation and understanding, the fact that the oral tradition is

taken as binding means that traditional Jews are servile and obedient, incapable of critical thinking, lacking creativity, etc. The mistake in this case is overlooking *the relevant background of beliefs*. The traditional Jew believes that the core of the oral tradition was also given at Sinai: the written and this part of the oral tradition have the same Author, the same antiquity, and hence the same authority. Accepting the word of the Creator of the Universe can hardly be regarded as a symptom of servility, etc. Hence this psychological interpretation of his behavior is wrong (as was already clear from our analysis of case #3).

(5) Jewish Law regulates behavior which would ordinarily be regarded as private. For example, smoking is prohibited on Shabbos. But a well-known doctrine decries legislating against "victimless crimes". Only behavior which affects other people should be the subject of legislation. The question will then be raised: Why does Jewish Law pass these limits? Theories of Jewish psychology, politics, and so on will be formulated in order to answer the question. But the question, and hence the subsequent theories, are based upon a false presupposition. For, *in the Jewish world view there is no such thing as a victimless crime*. The Jewish people is a single entity historically, and the actions of each Jew contribute to the historical fate of the nation and hence of other Jews. When the Babylonians took our people into exile, the saints marched beside the sinners. It is little comfort to the saints if the sinners protest that when they violated Shabbos, or brought unacceptable sacrifices, or neglected Torah study, they did so "in private". Imagine an orchestra playing a C major chord and the second oboist joining in with a C sharp. His protest that he did not cause anyone else to play off tune will not avail him. The orchestra is judged on the sum total of its efforts, and his note detracted from that sum. Similarly, the life of every Jew adds to (or subtracts from) the total Jewish effort and hence plays a role in the judgment of that effort. *Given this background belief, the comparison with victimless crimes is seen to be irrelevant*.

Finally, we consider the subtlest aspect of the background: values. Among our acquaintances are many who have beliefs different from ours, and we can easily imagine legal institutions unlike our own. With respect to fundamental values our life experience and imagination are much more uniform. We tend to assume that others share our values. However, that is sometimes incorrect. And when it is, it leads to misunderstanding their way of life.

(6) Every aspect of life is touched by Jewish Law. Not only civil and criminal matters, but clothing, food, sex, speech, and even sleep receive attention. Since at least some of these matters seem to be of no moral or spiritual relevance, why are they regulated? Theories of obsessive-compulsive behavior might make their appearance here. But it is the theories which are irrelevant, for, in the Jewish world-view, each of these "trivia" is in fact important. Imagine the director of an opera saying to one of the lead singers: "You've got the wrong hat on for that costume! Go back and change!" If you protest that the essence of opera is the music and the hat can't possibly affect the singer's tone, you will not be heard. An opera is a total theatrical event. Every element which touches the senses of the audience is regulated so as to contribute to the overall effect. This includes the staging, costumes, scenery (including live elephants to walk across the stage in *Aida!*), lighting, etc. To leave a "trivial detail" to chance is to pass up an opportunity to add to the overall theme. The Jewish perception of life has such an "esthetic" dimension. There is an overall theme and it is a central value to make the details of life help express and reinforce that theme. Given that value, Jewish Law is understood as no more compulsive than any well-organized coordinated effort to reach a goal, as is common in esthetics, sports, war, etc.

(7) Each person must decide the major focus (or foci) of his life. How is this decision made? Typically, by assessing which are the strongest talents and abilities which the person possesses, and then choosing a life-setting in which they will receive maximum

development. And yet, often an observant Jew willingly sacrifices his strongest talents in order to engage in activities at which he is mediocre at best. For example he may sacrifice practicing the violin (for which he has outstanding talent) to Talmudic study (in which he is merely mediocre). Or he may sacrifice his Talmudic study in order to support (both educationally and financially) the study of others even though they are far inferior to him in Talmudic ability. How shall we understand this phenomenon? There is another method for deciding one's life-focus: *assess social need* and then develop those capabilities which will make the largest contribution to that need (even if they are not your strongest capabilities). To take an (admittedly absurd) example: suppose a person could become the world's most outstanding water-skier, or a better-than-average social worker. Following the first strategy, he will be a water-skier: that is his strongest talent. Following the second strategy, he will be a social worker: the world benefits from (better-than-average) social workers far more than it does from the most accomplished water-skiers. Recall the social cohesion described in case #5. The Jewish world-view places a far higher value on one's social contribution than on one's "self-development". *Only in the light of that value can the sacrifice of stronger talents be understood.*

These illustrations of the Great Axiom of Anthropology reveal the tremendous burden placed upon anyone who would understand an action, practice or institution of classical Judaism: *the burden of competent scholarship.* Without doing the scholarly spadework (or conferring with those who have), the action, practice, or institution will not be the reality which is being evaluated, but a mere imaginary phantom. We might put the moral of our discussion as follows: *Uninformed experience is bound to be misunderstood.* And this suggests an important corollary: Academic study of Judaism without first-hand experience is also likely to be misunderstood. (This is the reason anthropologists do field studies.) Lectures (such as this one), books and other scholarly materials can *supplement but cannot substitute* for participation in key Jewish experiences. Only when the background required by the Great Axiom joins personal experience can we hope to understand traditional Judaism.

Questions & Answers

I don't agree with your example about human sacrifice. So what if they held some crazy belief that human sacrifice brings rain; that doesn't justify killing innocent human beings!

Of course it doesn't. But that wasn't the point of the example. The point was for us to understand *exactly what mistake* (by our lights!) they are making. Is it a matter of fundamentally different values, or a disagreement over a matter of fact? Imagine that we had the responsibility to try to change such a society. It would be crucial to know how *they* understood what they were doing so that we could choose a relevant strategy. Given their belief, they are morally very close to us. That is very different from imagining a society which did not value human life!

You mentioned Jewish Law's invasion into the private "victimless" areas of life. Now I can see how a belief in a God who judges the people as a whole, which then has consequences for the whole people, wipes out the idea of privacy in this sense. But what does it do for those of us who do not believe in that God?

Well, first it helps you understand those who do live by Jewish Law. They could agree *in theory* that private actions should not be regulated; but they believe that *in fact* there are no private actions, and hence no area of life is outside the scope of Jewish Law. (Of course, they are also free to *reject* the restriction against victimless crimes: there is no particular reason why *God* cannot legislate private behavior.) And second, perhaps it challenges you to re-think your position. If you *don't* believe in such a God, how do you explain Jewish history? Jewish survival in exile, the uniqueness of Judaism in ancient times, the impact of Jewish ideas and values on the rest of the world — if you analyze these and related ideas you may reconsider your present lack of belief.

I think you overstated the intellectual independence of traditional Jews. I find that they worship even their contemporary leaders, let alone those of previous "higher" generations. Their books are constructed by taking one central text and surrounding it by commentaries, like a king among his subjects. There may be disagreement among the leaders at one time, but it is almost unheard of to disagree with previous generations.

I think it would be important to know whether your remarks are based upon first-hand knowledge and experience, or mere hearsay. Have you read substantial portions of the *Shulchan Aruch* (Code of Jewish Law) with commentaries? Have you studies *Mikraos Gedolos*, or Alfasi's Code with the Me-or's critical glosses? If you had, you would know that your assumptions are false. The commentaries raise difficulties with the main text and feel free to disagree, even over a span of centuries. Let us remember, however, that a text attracts commentaries by distinguishing itself in an intense intellectual competition. The wide acceptance of a text by a hypercritical Jewish public testifies to the outstanding scholarship and intellect of its author. It is natural to treat such a text with respect (but see Raabad on Maimonides' code!). But respect never turns into blind obedience. Imagine contemporary physicists writing a commentary to Einstein's papers on relativity — what would you expect their attitude to be? As far as contemporary leaders are concerned, surely you didn't mean they are *worshiped*? I assure you, no one confuses them with the Creator of the universe! But they too have distinguished themselves in the intellectual-social-competition for Jewish leadership. That also entitles them to respect; but again, there is no blind obedience.

I don't understand the difference between developing my strongest talent and making the biggest social contribution. If I can be an outstanding dentist but only a mediocre accountant, isn't it obvious that society will benefit most by my becoming a dentist?

You are right for your example, but that is because you chose two professions which are of roughly equal social value. *In that case* the difference in value lies in the strength of the talent. But in other cases this is not true. If I could be the world's greatest billiards player, or an average policeman, will the greatest social contribution come from my playing billiards? I don't think so.

You mentioned that Jewish Law regulates every aspect of life, and you compared this to opera and sports where small details are also regulated. But those are only part-time activities. Jewish Law is life-long regulation. What happens to human spontaneity and creativity?

You are right that Jewish Law means lifelong regulation, and this distinguishes it from the examples I gave (though war is a closer approximation than opera or sports). But let's remember the point of the examples: regulation expresses the *significance* of the choices we make. My costume doesn't matter if I am practicing my part at home, but it does if I am part of a performance in front of an audience. Continuous regulation expresses the idea that *all* of our choices in *all* life situations are significant, and therefore cannot be left to chance. As for spontaneity, it depends what you mean. If you mean doing things for no other reason than you happen to feel like it at the moment, then indeed this has no place in traditional Jewish life. But if you mean using your intelligence to solve unique problems without explicit instructions, this is very common. The reason is that Jewish Law determines *goals* and *ideals* for action, but the strategies for achieving those goals will depend upon the individual's unique circumstances. Finding such strategies is an enormously creative process, and explains many of the differences in traditional Jewish lifestyles.

I didn't follow your last point about first-hand experience. What kinds of misunderstandings are likely to arise from academic study of Judaism?

I will give you an example. A Jewish college student once got hold of Dayan Grunfeld's *The Sabbath*. It was her first introduction to traditional Sabbath observance. Never having experienced or observed a traditional Sabbath, it struck her as distressingly restrictive. You can't answer the telephone, open up your mail, listen to the radio, turn the lights on or off, etc., etc. It struck her as a nerve-racking experience, constantly on the watch for dreaded infractions. Several months went by before she developed the courage to try it for herself. When she did (on a college campus with no support group — no one else was keeping Shabbos there), the experience was nothing like what she expected. Instead of "You can't..." she felt "I don't have to..." She felt *liberated* from the habits and reactions which often distract us from the more fundamental issues of life. (Can you not answer a ringing telephone, or pass by letters in your mailbox? Can you ignore the hourly news on the radio?) The twenty-five hours of Shabbos were for her an uninterrupted period of reflection on the deepest values and most fundamental goals of her life. She found this a precious experience. Now when she studies the myriad Shabbos prohibitions, she understands them as strategies to protect a unique quality of experience. This understanding could not have been achieved from book study alone. The same is true for other central Jewish events — a wedding, the Passover Seder, Yom Kippur, Simchas Torah; without personal participation they will not be understood.

Section II

Understanding

Mysticism,
Meaning
and Mitzvah

I. The rooster story: What does it mean to be human?

II. Mysticism — deeper dimension of reality

    A. In place of ordinary world — compare Plato's cave
    B. Real basis or ordinary world — compare science
    C. Jewish mysticism of type (B)

III. Jewish mystical picture

    A. Continuous creation — sparks of sanctity —
        R. Akiva on circumcision — world as unfinished —
        holiness potential
    B. Adam as androgynous — individual human
        incomplete
    C. Jewish people as single organism

IV. Meaning — context and relationships

    A. Examples — circle, "pain," G, hand signal
    B. Continuous creation — eating apple — sanctification
        of pleasure — Sabbath, holidays
    C. I and I, We, I relationships — marriage approximated
        the original Adam — functional integration
    D. Different roles within collective unity — choice of life
        — focus — responsibility for others' obligations

*V. Mitzvah — appropriate to total reality — objectivity —
analogy to medicine*

*VI. To be human — to be able to choose the meaning of your
life — intellect and will*

◈ Mysticism

T HE TALMUDIC SAGE HILLEL WAS ONCE ASKED
to explain all of Judaism while standing on one foot. If I
had been asked, and I were able to stand on one foot for
an hour, this is what I would have said.

R. Nachman of Breslev told the following story. Once there
was a king whose eldest son became mentally ill. The prince
disrobed, crawled under the dining room table, and crowed like a
rooster. He would eat only chicken feed by licking it off the floor;
he refused to speak; in short, he acted in all respects like a chicken.
The royal physicians and psychologists were powerless to cure
him. The king offered a reward and many tried, but there was no
change in the prince's condition. Finally, a rabbi offered his aid.

But the rabbi made a stipulation. "My therapy is a very radical one," he said, "and I must ask your promise not to interfere until its conclusion." The king consented. Immediately the rabbi disrobed, crawled under the dining room table with the prince, and crowed like a rooster! The two of them shared chicken-living for many days. One morning the prince awoke to find that the rabbi had put on a pair of pants. "What happened?" asked the prince. "I thought you were a chicken like me. Chickens don't wear pants! Why did you put on pants?" The rabbi replied: "You're right — I am a chicken like you. Does the fact that I have covered half of my body with cloth make me any less a chicken? Couldn't a chicken wear pants and still be a chicken?" The prince thought this over and had to agree that merely putting on pants would not threaten his status as a chicken. And so he put on his pants. The next morning the rabbi had his shirt on, and the same dialogue took place. "If a chicken puts on a shirt, is he any less a chicken?" And again the prince had to agree that a chicken could be a chicken and wear a shirt. And so he put on his shirt. By repeating the process the rabbi led the prince step by step back into normal human behavior, all the while reinforcing the prince's belief that he was still a chicken. The story ends with the prince completely "cured" — functioning in all respects like a normal person, though fully convinced that he is a chicken.

This story asks a question: What is it to be a human being? What is the essential difference between a person and a chicken? The clothes he wears? The chair on which he sits? The type of food he eats? His use of utensils? Every world view, every philosophy, every religion must answer this question. Its answer — its understanding of the essential nature of mankind — will contain its essential message for us. We are searching for Judaism's answer. To find it, we must first examine mysticism, meaning and mitzvah.

What is a mystic? We live in a world of tables and chairs, mountains and seas, stars and black holes, plants, animals and people, etc. This world of familiar (and sometimes not so familiar) objects is our reality. The mystic tells us that he is in touch with a dimension of reality quite different from the ordinary physical and human world. In his view, our perception of our normal environment is profoundly misleading. We are lead to think that the real world is composed of things we see, and nothing else. The mystic is convinced that his dimension is real, though quite different from what we perceive, and indeed *more real* than the world we think we know.

Thus far all mystics will agree. But on a further question they will split into two groups. What is the relation between the mystical reality and our ordinary world? (1) Some mystics hold our world to be a complete illusion. The ordinary physical world is *not real at all;* it is a dream, a fairy tale, which hides the true nature of reality (i.e. the mystical dimension) from us. This is the image in Plato's *Republic* [1] of men chained to the back of a cave, watching the shadows produced by dolls passing in front of a fire that is burning off to the side. To confront Reality for Plato requires being released from the cave and coming out into the sunlight. Then one will see an utterly new and different world. Such mystics typically preach withdrawal from the world — either physical withdrawal to the life of a hermit in a cave or on a mountaintop, or psychological withdrawal to a point of complete unconcern with what happens in the physical world.

(2) Other mystics hold our ordinary world to be real but not the *whole* reality — the mystical dimension is *also* real. Furthermore, the mystical dimension is a deeper reality; it underlies our ordinary world and determines its nature and what happens in it. Only through an understanding of the mystical dimension can one truly understand our ordinary physical world. Even though the mystical dimension itself is very different from the world we perceive, it reveals the true nature of that world. To understand this

---

1. Bk. VII. Although Plato did not intend this application of his image, it is apt nevertheless.

brand of mysticism, compare science. Consider the table in front of you. Look at it. Squeeze it. Pound it with your fist. In every respect it appears to be solid, continuous matter. It doesn't appear to have holes, gaps. And yet science tells us that the table is more than 99% empty space! (This ignores the subtlety of Quantum Mechanics, but the reader familiar with QM will see how to translate the point into its language.) The table seems quite peaceful, and yet science tells us that it is full of frantic activity. Its molecules are vibrating, and the electrons of its atoms are in constant motion. In short, science tells us that reality is very different from what our perception of the world reveals to our senses. (If we were not introduced to these ideas at an early age — if, say, we first heard them at 35 — we would regard them as absurd, going against all our experience.) But the scientist does not deny the reality of our ordinary world. He agrees that there is a real physical table in front of us. But he claims that we misunderstand what it really is. Only when we understand his deeper dimension of reality will we truly understand the table, because it is that deeper dimension which determines the nature of the table and what happens to it. The second type of mystic relates his mystical dimension to our ordinary world in the same way as does the scientist.

Judaism is a mystical religion of the second type. It possesses a vision of a deeper dimension of reality, but one which underlies our ordinary world and determines its nature. The point of understanding that vision is not to exit from the world, but rather to understand the world so that one can enter it and live in it intelligently. The value of the scientist's vision is that it enables us to understand our world and hence deal with it more successfully. The value of the Jewish mystical vision is precisely the same.

We will now examine — albeit briefly and superficially — three elements of that vision. In the next section we will see some of their consequences for our understanding of the world and our relation to it.

(1) You are probably aware of the well-known Jewish tenet that God created the world. It is less well-known that creation is not a one-time event in the past, but a continuous process at every moment.[2] God recreates the world at every instant. Were it not for the flow of Divine energy, all that exists would spontaneously lapse into nothingness. As a consequence, everything that exists partakes of God's Divinity and sanctity. This means that nothing that exists is inherently and irredeemably evil: indeed, nothing that exists is inherently and irredeemably *secular*. Each thing has a potential for holiness which will or will not be realized, depending upon how it is used. With respect to that potential the world exists in an unfinished state. Man is called upon to become a partner with God in completing the creation by realizing that potential.

A Roman asked[3] R. Akiva: "Whose actions are greater, those of God or those of man?" Anticipating that R. Akiva would reply piously that God's actions are greater, the Roman was prepared to challenge him with circumcision. The body is God's creation. Why then do Jews mutilate it by cutting off part of it, if God's actions are greater than man's? But R. Akiva answered that man's actions are greater than God's! And he proceeded to prove it. He put raw wheat and cake in front of the Roman and asked him which he would prefer to eat. When the Roman chose the cake, R. Akiva pointed out that God made the wheat, but man made the cake! That sufficed to stump the Roman, but we are not so easily put off. How can the wheat and the cake show the superiority of man's actions when man needs God's wheat in order to make the cake?! Furthermore, how do we make the cake? We need to thresh and winnow the wheat, grind the grain into flour, add other ingredients and apply heat so that various chemical changes will occur. All these processes depend upon the "laws of nature" as applied to the wheat, flour and other ingredients, each with its natural properties.

---

2. Maimonides, *Mishneh Torah*, Hilchos Yesodei HaTorah, I:1-3, and *Guide of the Perplexed*, I:69.

3. *Midrash Tanchuma*, Tazria, V.

But if God is constantly recreating the world, "nature" is just a name for His activity: He makes possible all of the processes in the production of the cake. Even "our" actions are largely due to God's help! How then can man's actions be superior to God's?

They can't, and that was not what R. Akiva meant. What he meant was that: the *end product* of man's actions is superior to the *end product* of God's actions. That is why God made wheat inedible and man-made cake edible. God has deliberately left the world in an unfinished state and invited man to finish it. Thus it is consistent for us to circumcise the body which God made; circumcision is our share in completing the creation of that body. In this respect, circumcision illustrates the Jewish attitude towards every part of the world. Each thing that exists is a *creation*; it owes its existence to a specific Divine decision. That connection to the Divine will gives it its sanctity-potential which can only be realized through appropriate human actions.

(2) We come now to the second element of the Jewish mystical picture. Adam, the first human being, was neither male nor female, but rather an androgynous being.[4] (According to a dissenting view, Adam was *planned* to be androgynous, but instead first a man and then a woman were created. What follows holds on either view.) Only later was Adam divided into two people, one male and one female. It follows that neither a man nor a woman is a complete being. Rather they are disconnected *parts* of a larger whole. If we could see deeply enough into their nature, we would perceive their incompleteness, just as we do with a half-finished puzzle. We would also see them as complementary, each contributing unique characteristics to an integrated unity. It would then be obvious that they were made for the sake of that unity: only by together forming the larger whole can they realize their individual potentials.

---

4. *Bab. Talmud, Eruvin,* 18a.

5. *Kuzari,* III:19; Ritba to *Rosh Hashana* 29a.

(3) The Jewish people (and ultimately all mankind) is viewed as a single integrated organism.[5] Individual Jews are viewed (at least in part) as the limbs and organs of this giant organism. Because of the linkage between them, what happens to each Jew has an effect upon every other Jew. Furthermore, the meaning and importance of what a Jew does is profoundly affected by his relation to the rest of the Jewish people. As a matter of metaphysical fact, no Jew is detached from the people of which he is a part. Take the human body as an analogy. All the limbs and organs are connected. An infection in my hand is not a private affair of the hand alone. The bloodstream will communicate the infection to the rest of the body, and hence the infection is a concern of the rest of the body as well. There is in addition a second sense in which the body functions as a unit. If my right hand signs a check that bounces, I cannot tell the claimant to leave me alone and collect from my right hand! For, even though it was my right hand whose motion produced the signature on the check, it is *I* who signed the check. The person signs, and becomes responsible, via the motion of his limb. Likewise, when a Jew acts, it is the Jewish people as a whole to whom the action is related. It is never a private affair of that individual.

So much for our glimpse of three elements of the Jewish mystical dimension. Now let us see how they transform our understanding of our ordinary world.

⮒ Meaning

Permit me to raise a very general, very abstract philosophical question. What is meaning? In the broadest sense, is meaning due to the intrinsic nature of a thing, its character in and of itself? Or is meaning due to the relations which hold between it and other things? Let's consider some examples.

What is the meaning of a circle? What is the meaning of "pain"? For the musicians among you: Is the note of G tonic or dominant? A driver extends his left arm out the window of his car with the forearm vertical and his hand bunched into a fist: What is the meaning of his gesture?

What is the meaning of a circle? Add rays and it symbolizes the sun; add eyes and a smile and it is a head; with the right additions, it can become a digit, or a position marker in a football diagram! The word "pain" either describes an unpleasant experience or a very common food, depending upon whether it is anEnglish or French world, and that will depend upon the context in which it is spoken or written. The note of G is tonic in a piece in G major and dominant in a piece in C major. If someone insists that he is not interested in the context in which "pain" was used, but wants to know *its own meaning* — he spelled it for us, after all, so we know what word he means — we can't answer his question. A word *has no meaning* apart from its linguistic context. Similarly a note cannot be tonic or dominant by itself. That aspect of its meaning consists in a relation to the rest of the music. The driver's gesture also will either signal a right turn or express his political views, depending upon the context. For example, if he is in England it must be a political gesture since only a passenger can put his left hand out the window! The examples indicate that *meaning is a function of relations between things.* Now, one of the consequences of a vision of the nature of reality is that it reveals new relations between the elements of our ordinary world, and hence *reveals new meanings.* For example, the scientist's vision associates both a burning match and rusting iron as cases of oxidation. Without knowledge of chemistry we might never associate one with the other. Now let us take each of the three facets of the Jewish vision sketched above and trace some of the relations and meanings it reveals.

(1) *Continuous creation.* You are about to eat an apple and want to do so fully conscious of the meaning of that act — i.e. of

its relations to the rest of the world. You want to *experience* the apple — you are from California! What goes through your mind? This apple came from a tree, which grew from a seed of an apple which came from an earlier tree which grew... and so on into the indefinite past. Shortly you will bite it and experience its pleasant taste and texture. You will swallow it and thus satisfy your hunger. Your body will digest it and it will help provide you with health, strength and energy, and these in turn will play a role in your future actions. You are crossing the plant and animal kingdom. With all this in mind you are conscious of the relations of your present bite to the past and future. You are conscious of its *meaning*. Now go ahead: take a bite!

But if we add the deeper vision of reality afforded by the Jewish mystical dimension, we are not quite ready to eat yet. That chain of apple-seed-tree-apple-seed-tree... does not extend into the "indefinite" past; it has a definite beginning at the creation. That beginning is the result of a caring Intelligence which planned that chain and all its consequences, including my possession of the apple which sits now in my hand. By constantly maintaining its existence even through my act of eating it and informing me that I may eat it, I am assured that it was intended for me and that there is some way that it can be used to enhance my life. The pleasant taste is a conscious gift of that Intelligence to me — I experience it not unlike a caress. So are health, strength and energy gifts, and I feel an indebtedness to that Intelligence which makes a claim on my use of those gifts. With all *this* in mind I am ready to take that bite.

(Judaism prescribes a blessing before one eats. One function of the blessing is to bring this added meaning to mind.[6] This is how Jewish mysticism is implemented practically.)

---

6. Jer. *Talmud, Kiddushim,* IV:12, end, see *P'nei Moshe*, Maimonides, *Mishneh Torah*, Hilchos Berachos, 1:4.

Just as the pleasant taste of the apple is a positive aspect of my relationship with God, so all physical pleasure can be incorporated into spirituality. It must be so: if God created the body with its capacity for pleasure and maintains its existence with His Divine creative energy, it must be sanctifiable.

Suppose God informed you that a certain day is to be set aside for contemplation of God and communion with Him. You are to design the activities of that day. What would you choose? If you choose prayer, study, fasting, introspection as your *only* paradigm, you are under the influence of non-Jewish thinking. Yom Kippur is not our only example of such a day. *Every Sabbath and every holiday is intended to be such a day.* The fact that they include feasting, song, community and family sharing and other pleasures is an expression of the Jewish idea that God can and *must be* reached through the physical.

(2) *Adam as male-female.* The idea of the first human being as an amalgam of man and woman radically transforms the meaning of marriage.

What is marriage? Ayn Rand speaks for many when she describes marriage as a purely contractual arrangement. Each party explicitly or implicitly agrees to deliver certain goods and services to the other. Any failure of performance gives the right to the other party to demand restitution or to dissolve the contract (and with it the relationship). Ideally an explicit contract should be drawn in the lawyer's office so that the legal rights of each are maintained.

Judaism perceives in marriage a far different meaning: *the reconstitution of the minimal human being.* Let's approach this idea in stages. The most superficial relationship between people (the Ayn Rand relationship) may be styled "I + I". Each person is to him/herself a completely self-interested "I". But each recognizes that there is another I, and that it is possible to form a mutually beneficial relationship with the other I. And so the association, the

"+", is formed. Each person is looking to the "+" for what it can give him/her. When it fails to deliver a minimum return for the investment made, he/she will dissolve it.

A step higher is the relationship expressed by "We". Each person feels that together they form a group which has an identity of its own. This group is more than the "sum" of its members; "+" does not do it justice. The interaction brings about a qualitatively new state of being and experience. The efforts of each are investments in the success of the group, and it is *its* success which justifies that investment.

However, there is still a failure of integration. The word "We" is plural: each person feels that the individual is allowed to retain his/her own identity intact while contributing to the group. This stage is analogous to a Beethoven sonata for violin and piano. Each part contributes its unique nature to a larger whole, but each part remains unchanged in itself throughout the contribution.

A still higher stage is reached when the "I" reappears, but this time it is a *single "I." There are no longer two separate beings contributing to a group, but a single being resulting from the integration of the former two.* Conventionally we may say that there are still a man and a woman who are parts of this new "I", but that will be as significant as pointing out that your body has its right and left sides as parts. One can distinguish these parts of the body if one wishes, but they are completely interdependent parts of one integrated whole. They cannot be separated without doing extreme violence to each. *Their identity and essence is to be parts of that larger whole.* At this stage, when the man and woman speak the word "I" they designate the same thing: the single whole of which each has become a part. (At the first stage when they each used "I" they designated two different things: he designated himself and she designated herself.) The vision of Adam as an integrated male-female teaches us that the meaning of marriage is an institution in which we may hope to approximate that creation.

Mysticism, Meaning and Mitzvah / 69

(3) *The organic unity of society.* Some people view nations as mere groups of people related to one another by proximity and/or common culture. Judaism sees the nation as a single individual in its own right, with particular people as its limbs and organs. Understanding one's identity is in part finding one's place in the national organism.

Some think that a vision of society as an organic unity means that all people are interchangeable — cookies cut from the same form. This is incorrect. The analogy of the body shows that the opposite is true. If each Jew is related to the Jewish people as a limb or organ to a body, then we expect each Jew to be different in nature, capabilities and function with respect to the nation. Just as thirty-two hearts sewn together do not make a functioning body, so a group of interchangeable people do not make a nation. Just as a body requires a heart, eyes, toenails, hair follicles, a spleen, etc., each with its distinct structure and function, so the nation requires people with varied talents and strengths. When a person identifies his unique ability and finds the appropriate position in the nation to put it to use, this becomes part of the meaning of his life.

This task of identification is performed in part by Jewish law. A Jew is either a Cohen (priest) or a Levi (helper to the priests) by heredity. This means that God has endowed him with certain special talents and has designated the role he is to play in society to make maximum use of those talents. Beyond the legal categories, the infinite individual differences which comprise the uniqueness of each person's life challenge him to find his own place in the nation.

Each person must choose the theme of his life — to what vocation or life's work will he dedicate himself? How is this decision made? There are at least two ways. (1) One may assess one's talents and choose that life project which develops the strongest. If I have the ability to be a mediocre violinist, a better-than-average dentist, and an outstanding architect, I will choose to be an architect. (2) One may choose to develop those talents whose exercise will realize the greatest value. If I have the ability to be a very great water-skier and a reasonably good social worker, I will now choose to be a social worker. Even the modest contribution to human happiness made by a good social worker far outweighs the contribution of the greatest of water-skiers. (Think of the Dutch boy who put his finger in the hole in the dike. Perhaps he was on his way to play a violin concert that only he could give. Putting his finger in the hole did not express his greatest talent; should he have gone on?) Given the vision of organic unity which Judaism possesses, (2) is an important part of the strategy for planning one's life.

Here is a moral dilemma. A and B have obligations which accidently conflict with one another. If A does what he is obligated to do, then B will not be able to fulfill his obligation, and this conflict between A and B is no one's fault. (Imagine that A and B share a car and that each has promised a ride to someone, A at 3:00 and B at 4:00. If A leaves at 3:00 he cannot be back by 4:00.) How should the conflict be resolved? In particular, suppose that it is up to A to make the decision: he has the power to fulfill his obligation or not, and B cannot stop him. How should A make his decision? There are at least two ways. (1) A may say: "I have my own obligation to honor. The fact that B will be prevented in honoring his is no fault of mine — the conflict is accidental. Nor have I any right to take it into account. I don't have an obligation to see that B's obligations get fulfilled — that is B's business. Furthermore, B's failure will not be his fault either. His failure will be due to circumstances beyond his control. There would be no point in my deliberately violating my responsibility in order to avoid his accidental failure to fulfill his." (2) A may say: "There are two obligations which need attention, and only one will and can be fulfilled. The only relevant consideration is that the best action be performed, and that depends upon the weight of the two responsibilities. The fact that one is mine and the other belongs to someone else doesn't affect the decision at all. I have to act exactly as I would if I were personally responsible for *both* obligations. If it is clear in some objective sense that his weighs more than mine, then I must deliberately violate mine so that he can fulfill his." (Imagine that A has promised to drive a friend to the tennis courts and B has promised to drive his mother to the hospital for an operation.)

Which method should A use to make his decision? To the extent that he perceives society as an organic unity, he should use (2). Insofar as A is part of such a society, his chief obligation is to help that society perform optimally. Which limb does the performance is not crucial; maximizing the product is. This element of the Jewish vision introduces a new concept of social responsibility as expressed in (2).[7]

Eating an apple, physical pleasure, marriage, choosing a vocation, inter-personal moral dilemmas — all are part of our everyday lives. Just as their meanings are transformed by these elements of Jewish mystical dimension, so is the rest of life transformed by the totality of the Jewish vision.

⇜ Mitzvah

The root meaning of the word "mitzvah" is "command". But our discussion suggests another definition: *A mitzvah is an action which is appropriately related to the totality of reality.* Reality consists of our ordinary world plus the mystical dimension. An action has relations and consequences in terms of both levels. If we could see the total picture, we would understand the meanings of the various alternatives open to us and we would then know what

---

7. *Bab. Talmud, Shabbos* 4a, *Eruvin* 103b, *Pesachim* 59a, *Chagiga* 2b, *Gittin* 41b (*Tos.* "kofim").

to choose. A mitzvah is an action which the Author of the total reality chose in order to relate ideally to that reality.

One need not be aware of the meaning of an action in order for that action to have that meaning. You don't know that you are making yourself a millionaire when you purchase the winning lottery ticket; until twenty years ago people didn't know that they were killing themselves when they smoked; many idol worshipers didn't know that their religious performances were at best devoid of spiritual value. A mitzvah is *the* action which is best related to the total reality not because it *seems* best or *feels* best, but because the nature of that reality determines it to be best. (Compare: This is the best medicine for the ailment not because it seems best or feels best, but because the nature of the ailment and the medicine determine it to be best.) Jewish law is a codification of these best actions. By following that law, an individual can be sure that he is acting as well as he can, even if he does not understand in detail how and why those actions are best. (Compare: by following the doctor's regimen of diet, rest and medicine you can be sure that you are doing the best for your health, even if you do not understand in detail the physiology and pharmacology which make those actions best.)

This is not to say that understanding and consciousness of the meaning of our actions is unimportant. The ultimate point of those best actions is to bring a person into a relationship with God. This is a person to Person relationship; the actions which express it are not mere movements of the body, but expressions of the personality in a conscious relationship. The more understanding one possesses, and the more one brings that understanding to bear on one's actions so as to maximize their *conscious* meaning, the deeper that relationship will be. But one does not wait for that understanding before one chooses the best action. (Compare: One does not wait to attend medical school before one chooses to follow the doctor's advice.)

Mysticism, Meaning and Mitzvah / 73

Finally, we can return to the question with which we started. What is it to be a human being? One way of putting the Jewish answer is this: To be human is to have the ability to *choose the meaning of your life.* You remember that meaning is a matter of relations and consequences. The meaning of a life is determined by its connections to the rest of history. Imagine a stream. By studying its flow you can predict that if you enter the stream at a certain spot and in a certain way, you will change its flow in a specific manner. History is like that stream. By studying the past and the probable course of the future, you can predict that if you act in a specific way at a specific place and time, you will affect the future course of history in a specific manner. That effect, together with its relations to the rest of the past and the future, is the meaning of your life. The uniqueness of man lies in his *intellect* which enables him to envision the meanings of the various life courses open to him, and in his *will* which enables him to choose one of those life courses. The essential characteristic of a human being is *the ability to choose the meaning of his life.* Only in the light of the total reality — including the mystical dimension — can that choice be well made.

Questions & Answers

LEVEL ONE

You said that God is continuously recreating the world out of nothing. If so, how do we understand the "six days of creation" after which God rested? Isn't every day a day of creation?

During the six days of creation, *new* things came into existence — new *types* of things — earth, water, plants, animals, man. From then on God created the same *types* of things, although each *individual* object is new every instant since it is recreated from nothing each instant.

You mentioned that physical pleasure can be incorporated into spirituality, but you didn't explain how we can do this!

Well, I did mention experiencing the pleasant taste of the apple as God's caress. But, since your question touches on one of Judaism's most fundamental ideas, let's consider some other examples.

There are four ways to eat a steak. (1) You have just finished a delicious and filling dinner when someone knocks on your door. You open the door and see a friend with a covered tray. "Happy Birthday!" he shouts as he uncovers the tray to reveal a two-inch-thick sirloin steak, smothered in onions. But you are full from dinner — what to do? Then you remember some Roman history, go into the bathroom and put your finger down your throat and ... you re-appear, thank your friend, and enjoy the steak, thinking: *"That's* the value of a good education!" (2) You have been out mountain climbing and are exhausted and famished. There is a knock on the door, "Happy Birthday!" etc. as before. (3) You are marrying off your daughter. The guests have been invited, and you are serving for the meal two-inch steaks, etc. (4) Imagine a country whose ruler is exceedingly wise and benevolent, and who is loved and revered by all his subjects. (I realize this requires a lot of imagination.) He is giving a dinner party for his twenty-five most intimate friends, and you are invited. When you arrive, they serve two-inch steaks, etc. What are the differences between these different ways of eating the steak?

In the first, the human being has made himself even sub-animal. Animals eat to satisfy their hunger; they do not regurgitate in order to enjoy unneeded food. In the second, the real need for food makes the eating reasonable and responsible. And then, there is no reason in Jewish terms not to enjoy it. In the third, the physical pleasure of the steak is integrated into the celebration of your daughter's wedding. In the fourth, the steak is a tiny part of the immense joy of closeness to your beloved king. (The intended analogy is the relationship of the Jewish people to God.) One way to spiritualize physical pleasure is to make it part of a larger context whose overall meaning is spiritual.

Jews make blessings before they eat. The Talmud tells us that without the blessing we do not have permission to eat God's food: eating without a blessing is stealing. So most people *make the blessing in order to eat.* Some people reverse the order. They are looking for ways to relate to God, ways to enter into dialogue with Him. A blessing is one way to do this. "Blessed are You, God our God, King of the universe, Who creates the fruit of the tree." I would like to say those words, but unless I eat a fruit I cannot. Does anyone have an apple? An apple for the blessing! Here physical pleasure is a means to the God-connection of the blessing.

These are just a couple of examples of how Judaism spiritualizes pleasure. I hope they show you at least that such a thing is possible.

In describing the incompleteness of the individual, and the fact that men and women are complementary to one another, you made it sound as if everyone ought to be married. Is there no place for singles in Judaism?

Of course, an unmarried person's life can have value in Jewish terms. Many mitzvos can still be done, including those by which one can be of service to others. Nevertheless, there are dimensions of life — dimensions of personal fulfillment as well — which are unrealized for singles. In marriage, a person is challenged to develop levels of personality which otherwise would atrophy, and this is even more true of childbearing and rearing. Suffice it to say that all the great Jews of the past married and had children; apparently that is the norm for Jews (in addition to the mitzvos involved).

Your description of forming the single "I" in marriage was very abstract. Can you give any practical examples of how this idea is applied?

It would really take a whole session to adequately explain the single "I" and its applications, but perhaps an example will help. Here is a problem which arises in every marriage from time to time. Your spouse starts relating some incident of the day and you think: "Oh no! Not again! This is the nth time she/he is telling me about this sort of thing. How boring!" How do you deal with this situation? There are two common schools of thought. (1) Marriage requires consideration and self-sacrifice. Hear your spouse out even if it is boring. (2) Marriage is based upon honesty and frank, open communication. If it's boring, tell your spouse: "It's boring! I can't stand it! etc." If you choke down your frustration, it will surface in some other interaction, and that will be worse.

Now despite the popularity of these two approaches, I think they are both mistaken. The content of the message may indeed be boring, but you are not listening to the *message*; you are listening to *him/her*. Constructing the single "I" means a commitment to sharing and building communication. You need to know what your spouse is thinking and feeling *now*, even if it is the same as it was before. A doctor doesn't lose interest in a patient's condition just because it is stable. Attuning yourself to what is going on in your spouse's life is a full-time commitment, no matter how varied or uniform that life is.

I was surprised by your description of the essence of being human. Intelligence and will, as used in choosing the meaning of one's life, are not particularly religious. Couldn't a non-believer have said the same? I was expecting something about the soul.

You are right — the real essence of mankind lies in the human soul. But for us, that is just a word. What is the soul? In Jewish terms we cannot hope to define the soul's essence because it shares God's transcendence. We can only know it by what it does. Therefore I chose its two most important abilities in their relationship to our lives to indicate the functioning of the human soul.

Questions & Answers

LEVEL TWO

The idea that God is constantly recreating the world is supposed to imply that everything has a potential for sanctity which man is challenged to realize. Nevertheless, there are certain things which Jewish Law requires to be destroyed — offerings to idols, for example. The fact that they have to be destroyed seems to indicate that they don't have any sanctity-potential, even though their existence is dependent upon God's will just like everything else.

Even something which Jewish Law requires to be destroyed still has sanctity-potential, and *it is precisely its destruction which realizes that potential.* This is somewhat comparable to food which realizes its life-sustaining potential through its own destruction. Of course in the case of food *we see* the potential being realized through the destruction, whereas with the idol offerings we do not see this. But the Torah is telling us that the connection exists. There is also a deeper *motif* here: The destruction of evil is a revelation of God's unity and His total control of the world.[8]

---

8. *Michtav MeEliyahu,* v. 3, pp. 24-25, 151-152; *Messilas Yesharim (Path of the Just),* chap. 26; *Daas Tevunos (The Understanding Heart),* pp. 10-36 (Heb. Ed.).

You made an analogy with science in order to explain your second type of mystic. You seem to have forgotten the chief virtue of science: all of its theories can be proved by experiment and observation. Your "mystical dimension" by contrast is something which one must take on pure faith.

I think you are overstating the case a little. Scientific theories can *sometimes* be *disproved* by experiment and observation, but can never be *proved* by them. However, a full discussion of science will have to wait for another occasion. And your reference to "pure faith" on the Jewish side is also inaccurate. Jews have never been asked to believe in the irrational. At every point in Jewish history there was enough evidence to warrant Jewish belief. It requires a long and careful discussion to specify the evidence exactly and explain the warrant, but at no time have Jews taken an irrational "leap of faith" into the unknown.

I have a question on a different topic. Your discussion of the organic unity of society concerns me. I understand that my individuality need not be compromised: the nation may make appropriate use of my unique abilities. But does not life have any individual meaning apart from the role I play vis-a-vis the group?

It does have individual meaning. By stressing the collective side I meant only to *include* it as *one* dimension of life's meaning. For Judaism, life has *both individual and collective* meaning. It is very interesting how this emerges from the legal sources, and only those sources can resolve the inevitable conflicts which arise between one's obligations in these two areas.

I didn't follow your definition of "mitzvahh". You

said that if we could see the total reality, including the
mystical dimension, we would know what to choose. You
used the analogy of the doctor to imply that one course of
action is objectively right, given the circumstances. But
don't people sometimes disagree concerning what is right
even when they agree on all the facts? Didn't Hume argue
that one can't get from an "is" to an "ought", i.e. that no
mere description of objective fact can imply any moral
conclusion?

Your question is excellent, and it will be answered fully when we discuss the Jewish foundations of morality at length. For now, notice first that when people disagree morally in spite of agreeing on all the facts, this is usually due to a *conflict* of values. Both parties share the same values, but resolve the conflict differently. If, for example, some social good can be achieved by abridging someone's property rights, people may differ concerning which is more important (the good or the rights) while admitting that both are important. What would happen in a case where all the values were on one side? Suppose that a small child is in danger of injury which will cause immense suffering, and the danger can be averted with virtually no expenditure of time, effort or resources. Will people disagree even in a case like that? Now our view is that the total reality will reveal that all values are served best by living in accordance with Jewish Law. Seeing that, the choice is dictated by the facts. This also answers Hume: we are starting with certain undisputed values which, together with the facts, dictate the "objectively right" choice. There is no attempt to derive an "ought" from an "is".

I don't understand the idea of two levels or dimen-
sions of reality, one "more real" than the other. If science
is our paradigm, surely atoms and sub-atomic particles

are not another "level" or "dimension" of reality. They are simply the smallest parts of the objects of our world. Of course, by understanding the parts we understand the wholes they compose, but this does not mean that the parts are "more real" than the whole.

You are right. Strictly speaking, we cannot say that one thing is more real than another. It is a matter of revealing the true nature of our world. The physicist says that the table is really such-and-such collections of particles, and through his description we can understand how the table does what we observe. Similarly, calling the mystical dimension "more real" just indicates that it is the underlying structure of our world, and hence the key to understanding that world.

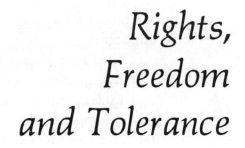

Rights,
Freedom
and Tolerance

I. Rights as political foundation

    A. Inalienable rights — at least to non-interference
    B. Political freedom
    C. Social tolerance
    D. Negative rights vs. claims on social support

II. Limitations in practice

    A. Social needs limit rights — utilitarianism as anti-liberal principle
        1. Graduated income tax protection
        2. Compulsory education
        3. Consumer protection
        4. Integration
    B. Either utility overrides rights, or rights are justified by utility
    C. Freedom and tolerance only for the irrelevant or the uncertain

III. The Torah Viewpoint — obligations replace rights

    A. No word for rights
    B. Practical differences
        1. Rights can be waived
        2. Who may redress wrongs
    C. No property rights — "The earth is the Lord's . . ." — miser vs. indiscriminate giver
    D. No bodily rights — abortion vs. self-mutilation
    E. No rights to life — life is continuous gift
    F. Rights → infinite worth of *any* human will; obligations → value in appropriate exercise of will in relation to God

ᴥ§ Rights, Freedom and Tolerance

"WE HOLD THESE TRUTHS TO BE SELF-evident, that all men are created equal, that they are endowed by their Creator with certain inalienable rights, that among these are life, liberty and the pursuit of happiness — that to secure these rights, governments are instituted among men, deriving their just powers from the consent of the governed..."

These words from the American Declaration of Independence are the foundation of American political theory. Our present interest is the stress placed on rights — *inalienable* rights — to life, liberty and the pursuit of happiness. The sole function of government, according to the Declaration, is to secure these rights for the governed. These rights are inalienable; under normal conditions a citizen cannot lose these rights.

This emphasis upon rights leads to two conclusions, one political and one social. The political conclusion is the value of freedom. Laws and institutions should be structured so as to maximize individual freedom so that the exercise of rights is protected. The social consequence is the value of tolerance. A social system which gives prominence to individual rights and freedom may be expected to result in considerable variation in life-style. In order to preserve social harmony, people must accept others' differences.

The rights described generally in the Declaration of Independence and guaranteed in the Constitution have one very important characteristic in common: They are *rights to non-interference*. Life, liberty and the pursuit of happiness; free exercise of religion, speech, press, assembly, petition; security of person and property against searches and seizures; abolition of slavery; the right to vote — all are designed to allow the individual freedom of action unhampered by governmental interference. The right to life, for example, prohibits government and private citizens from arbitrarily eliminating their opponents. The right to pursue happiness prohibits government from imposing its idea of happiness, or its preferred means of achieving happiness upon unwilling individuals. Security of property protects the individual against theft or governmental seizure. These have been called negative rights — rights to be left alone, to do as one pleases. Of course, all these rights are limited by the need to respect others' exercise of the *same* rights. One person cannot use his right of free speech to shout down someone else. One important function of government is to devise rules which allow for maximum exercise of rights to free action by all members of society, and to enforce those rules.

Understanding these rights negatively is important, because sometimes a quite different idea is expressed using the same word.

We may hear of a "right" to free education, to a minimum wage or a minimum standard of living, or to free medical care for the indigent. It should be clear that these examples are worlds away from those of the Declaration and Constitution. The "right" to a free education is not a matter of *non-interference* or of being left alone to do as one pleases. On the contrary, *it is a "right" to claim society's support* for a service. Since society is composed of one's fellow citizens, it means *a claim to their resources* for that service. (Of course the taxes to pay for schools will be levied on the society generally. But there will be those too poor to pay, and still their children will get free schooling. And in general the amount paid in taxes will not be proportional to the number of children in school.) The same is true for a minimum wage, standard of living and medical care: All are claims on someone else's resources for those services.

The importance of the difference between the last-mentioned *claims*, on the one hand, and rights to non-interference on the other, can be illustrated as follows. Imagine a foreign policy decision to aid only those countries which do not violate basic human rights. The intention is to exclude dictatorships and tyrannies from U.S. aid. Of course if a government imprisons or exiles its political opponents, censors newspapers, forbids opposition parties, or prohibits the practice of certain religions, it is clear that it does not qualify for aid. However, suppose the complaint against a government is that it does not provide free schooling, or social security, or free medical services to the poor. Shall we say that it violates basic human rights — that it is a dictatorship or tyranny because it does not provide these services to its citizens? Clearly this is going too far. We may feel that it is good for governments to provide these services. We may even feel that they ought to do so, and that their social policy is morally deficient if they do not. None of this qualifies them as dictatorships or tyrannies. The reason is that so far they are not interfering with their citizens' rights to be left alone and live as they please.

Thus the basic human rights which are inalienable and form the foundation of government are negative rights of non-interference. Notice that we are not speaking of *legal* rights. The Declaration of Independence was meant to justify removing one form of government and replacing it with another. Rather, it is *moral* rights that are at stake. The Declaration asserts that people are *morally entitled* to exercise all those rights necessary to insure life, liberty and the pursuit of happiness. Therefore a government's record concerning these rights can be used to justify or criticize that government.

Considering how fundamental these rights are, one might expect them to have top priority in our legal system. Surprisingly, this is not the case. There is a different value for the sake of which rights are regularly sacrificed. This value is *social welfare*. Rights are restricted, or even denied, when their exercise is seen to jeopardize the social good. I will first argue for this claim via examples. Then I will mention a possible explanation. This will be followed by an examination of Jewish sources on the subject of rights.

Here are four examples of the sacrifice of rights for the sake of social welfare.

(1) *The graduated income tax*. The more money you earn, the higher a percentage of your income is taken in taxes. What is the justification for this practice? More particularly, how is it related to government's prime responsibility to protect our rights?

The simplest rationale for taxation is payment for services rendered. The government collects garbage, builds roads, provides security, etc. and deserves to be paid for those services. How much should each person pay? Presumably, in proportion to how much he uses. How, then, does a person earning $100,000 pay, say $50,000 in tax, while someone earning $20,000 may pay $2,000, and someone earning $10,000 may pay nothing at all?! Clearly the first person is not getting twenty-five times as much governmental service as the second (though he will get something more — he probably produces more garbage, uses the roads more, has more property to protect, etc.), and the third is getting a free ride. The first person's tax money is being used in part to subsidize the services of the others. How does this relate to the rights of the people involved?

The first person's property rights are being violated. His money is taken without his consent and awarded to someone else. In terms of rights this cannot be justified. His liberty, pursuit of happiness and security of property are not being respected at all. It does not help that the taxes are being decided upon democratically. That only makes them the will of the majority. The fundamental "inalienable" rights are supposed to protect the individual against the power of government — even democratic governments. If the individual does not agree to subsidize the services of the poor, the law of the majority amounts *morally* to violation of his property rights.

Of course, the graduated income tax does serve an important purpose: People are afforded certain necessities even though they cannot pay for them. Those who are paying the bill can far better afford it than those who pay less or not at all. Without the graduated income tax, government revenues would be severely restricted. The resulting reduction of government services would lower the quality of life for the majority of the community. All this means that the graduated income tax may be morally correct. But its correctness can only be argued by placing communal quality of life ahead of property rights. Social welfare thus takes precedence over the "inalienable" rights of the individual.

(2) *Compulsory education.* Imagine a family which has decided that its children shall not learn how to read. ("It is bad for your eye muscles, all that back-and-forth motion," they say. Or perhaps they don't want to "prejudice" their children about reading and will let them make their own decision as adults.) In all democratic societies of which I am aware this choice is not open to

parents. You don't have to send your children to school — you can educate them at home if you wish. But a certain minimum curriculum dictated by the state must be followed. Where are this family's rights to non-interference, to the pursuit of happiness as they understand it?

Of course, the rationale of the law is not a mystery: the child's life will be happier, more productive, etc., if he learns to read. He will be a better informed citizen and contribute more to his community. Literacy is the key to great value for him and his society. We may agree that a law making literacy compulsory is well justified morally by contributing to that value. But we must remember that our agreement is based upon putting that value above the family's free decision for its children's education. This is again a sacrifice of rights for the sake of (the child's and society's) welfare.

(3) *Consumer protection.* In the United States it is illegal to sell unpasteurized milk. You are a farmer with a pail of fresh milk. I decide I would like to try some and offer you fifty cents for a glass. It is a matter of two consenting adults trading their private property. How in the name of rights to non-interference can the state forbid this? It cannot. The real rationale is in terms of health — unpasteurized milk can cause disease. Thus our freedom and property rights are again sacrificed for the sake of social welfare.

(4) *Integration.* I am the sole owner and operator of a luncheonette in Mobile, Alabama. I like to serve people over six feet tall with blue eyes whose last names begin with "L". The government tells me: "You cannot decide whom you will serve. *We* will decide, and we are telling you that you must serve anyone who wishes to be served." Now we understand that a social policy of non-discrimination leads to mutual understanding, harmony, cooperation and so on. But it must be recognized that to achieve these goals, the rights of the individual are being sacrificed. The same holds for forced busing of children to integrated schools. This

practice may also further those social goals, but clearly the rights of families to determine the education of their children are being violated.

These examples illustrate the priority of social welfare over rights. They are not atypical. The cancer patient who wants to try laetril, the driver who doesn't want to wear a seat belt, the American who wants to visit Cuba, the home owner who wants to build a two-story Tudor castle in a neighborhood zoned for one-story ranch houses — all suffer restriction or loss of rights (even the right to protect one's *life* as one sees fit, in the case of laetril) for the sake of some social good. It seems, then, that we have a general principle: Whenever the exercise of a right will adversely affect social welfare, we deny permission. How can this be explained?

Briefly, there are two possibilities. (1) Social welfare is an independent moral principle having greater moral weight than rights. (2) Rights themselves are only justified insofar as they contribute to social welfare, and thus in a case of conflict, rights must be sacrificed. If (1) is correct, then rights are severely demoted in the moral order of things. The statement of the Declaration of Independence that "...to secure these rights, governments are instituted among men..." surely gives the opposite impression. And if (2) is correct the situation is even worse: Morally there is *only* welfare; rights are only *means* to that end. It can be argued that John Stuart Mill, the supposed champion of rights and liberty, accepts the second explanation. We can go into this during the question period, if any of you are interested. For the present, we will note two consequences of the pre-eminence of social welfare for the elements of political theory with which we started.

First, the idea of tolerance needs revision. After all, in each of the examples above *we are not tolerating the values and decisions of those individuals* (not to subsidize the poor, not to teach their children to read, to buy/sell unpasteurized milk, to serve only certain people in his luncheonette). It seems that in practice we are only tolerant of others' differences when either (1) those differences have no practical importance, or (2) we don't think we know the truth. If someone wears a different style of clothing, or believes there are twelve planets in the solar system, we tolerate him because his differences have no practical effect. If someone wants his children to eat only macrobiotic foods, we tolerate him because we have no knowledge that such a diet is detrimental. But if both (1) and (2) fail — if we think that we know the truth about a matter of practical importance — then we enlist the power of the state to force people to conform to our ideas.

Second, certain typical debates need to be re-evaluated. Take pornography, for example. Defenders of the unrestricted distribution of pornography often cast the issue in terms of rights — rights to free speech, trade, the pursuit of happiness, etc. But how will they distinguish these rights from the right to sell unpasteurized milk? In terms of the "inalienable" rights concerned, there is no difference. In both cases, freely consenting adults wish to exchange their private property. To interfere with either exchange is to impose society's values upon individuals who do not accept those values. The *real* issue is one of social welfare. Unpasteurized milk is dangerous to health, and public health is a universally recognized value. Defenders of pornography don't recognize any public value which they are compromising. (This attitude is changing; certain feminist groups now recognize the detrimental effect of pornography on attitudes towards women.) Thus it is not a debate concerning rights in principle. Rather the debate is over the existence of a social value with which the rights conflicts. All parties to the debate agree that if there *is* such a conflict, the rights will have to be sacrificed.

Having put rights into a general perspective, let's turn to Jewish sources. Here we find something fascinating: Classical Jewish sources lack the very concept of rights! Indeed, there is no classical Hebrew or Aramaic *word* for rights. (In modern Hebrew a word meaning "acquittal," "merit" or "benefit" has to do double duty.) Apparently, the system of Jewish morality has no place for rights. How are we to understand this omission?

First we must examine exactly what difference it makes to omit rights from a moral system. Notice that rights create corresponding obligations. For example, my right to life obligates you not to kill me. This watch is my property. That means that you are obligated not to steal it or destroy it. My right to freedom of movement means that you may not lock me up or impede my progress (unless you are exercising *your* right to free movement). Now imagine a moral system based on *obligation* which has all those obligations which corresponds to rights. Is anything lost if we don't have the rights themselves? Perhaps they are equivalent to the corresponding obligations?

I think this suggestion is wrong in at least two respects. (1) The detailed conditions of obligations based upon rights will differ from those of obligations arising from another source. (2) The justifications of the two types of obligations differ widely. Let's take these points in turn.

Consider my watch again. In a rights system, your obligation not to steal or destroy my watch is subject to my waiver. If I waive my right — if I invite you to take my watch or destroy it — your obligation not to do so disappears. The same is true for my right to life. If your obligation not to kill me is based solely on my right to life, then my waiver releases you from your obligation and you are morally permitted to kill me. Now contrast this with a situation in which there are no rights at all, and the obligations come from a different source. Let's say that you have promised George not to take or destroy my watch. In this case my giving you permission to do so is irrelevant: I can't release you from your promise to George. Similarly, if your obligation not to kill me is due to God's commandment forbidding murder, my willingness to die cannot release you from that obligation. Thus the appropriateness of waiver is one distinction between the two types of obligations.

A second distinction concerns redress of failure to honor those obligations. In a rights system, if someone destroys my watch, it is morally appropriate for me to take action. In this case, it is I who am the victim, and therefore it is up to me to seek redress. However, if the obligation is created by a promise to George, then my action is no longer appropriate. Only George can redress the crime of destroying my watch. The reason is that it is George who is the moral victim since it is the promise to him which has been broken.

Waiver and redress are thus two differences in the conditions of the two types of obligations. There may be other differences of detail, but we will turn now to illustrations from Jewish Law. There are three areas in which rights are fundamental for our lives: life, bodily security and property. How will these be affected if Jewish Law does not recognize these rights?

Let's take property first. In Jewish terms there cannot be property rights because, strictly speaking, there is no property. No human being owns anything. "The earth is the Lord's..." What we call "property" is only a matter of supervision or custodianship. Certain things are under our control, but they are not truly ours. Imagine visiting a factory. You see someone unlock the doors, assign the workers to their tasks, signal rest periods, pay the workers, and lock up. Is he the owner of the factory? No — the owner lives in Beverly Hills and visits the factory twice a year! You observed the *foreman* who runs the factory for the owner. Similarly, our job is to use whatever objects are in our control in the service of the Owner. This means that we never give *our* money to charity — we disburse money from the Owner's account to charity. Consider this question: Which is worse, to deny money to the poor, or to give money to a faker who doesn't need it? From this perspective there is a sense in which they are the same. If we give to the faker, there is less money in the charity account for those who are really poor. Either way the poor suffer. Of course, to say that we *own* nothing does not permit *stealing* — there are obligations not to interfere with another's custodianship. But our attitude towards "our possessions" is profoundly transformed.

The same holds for our bodies. They too are God's creations. This means that we have no bodily rights. As you may well imagine, this position has many consequences. For example, consider abortion. I don't want to get into all the details of this difficult issue; only one point concerns me. How does the debate usually go? At some point between conception and birth, the fetus becomes a human being. After that point, abortion amounts to killing a human being, and is permissible only under the most severe circumstances. Before that point the fetus is merely a part of the mother's body. As such it is subject to her decision; just as she could decide to cut off her little finger, so she can decide to abort the fetus. (The debate then centers on defining the crucial point in time.) Now in Jewish thinking there is a false assumption here. True, aborting the fetus is equivalent to cutting off a finger. But are you allowed to cut off your finger? Jewish Law says not. God has decreed a prohibition against self-mutilation (Of course this law has exceptions, and some of them apply to abortion as well.) Thus abortion *at will* is unacceptable in Jewish terms since our bodies are not our possessions. Again, having said this, assault and battery are ruled out by *obligations* not to injure others. But this is worlds away from a concept of bodily rights.

Finally, consider life itself. Even here Judaism denies rights. Certainly vis-a-vis God we have no right to life. The reason is that life is a gift which God dispenses, moment by moment. The fact that God created me and has sustained my life this long does not give me a right to *more* life. Imagine that every morning at 7:30 a certain person hands you ten dollars. This goes on for years. Then one morning he doesn't appear. When you ask him later, he replies: "The free ride is finished, I'm not giving you any more." Has he violated your rights? All you can do is thank him for his previous generosity. This holds true even if you used the money he gave precisely as the donor wished. Life is exactly parallel. Even if I have lived exactly as God wanted, that merely justifies the life He already gave. It gives me no claim on life in the future.

Of course the lack of a right to life does not permit murder. God has prohibited that. But it does affect the question of suicide. If murder is ruled out because it violates our right to life, then we can waive that right and end our own lives. If God's law governs life, then suicide depends upon His will. In fact, it is forbidden.

These examples illustrate the profound differences between our ordinary way of thinking and the conceptions of Jewish Law. Ultimately the differences are rooted in a fundamentally different world-view. God as Creator and Sustainer of all existence, and communion with Him as the goal of life — these ideas are the ground of the Jewish morality of obligation.

Finally let's consider the issue of justification.

A rights system expresses a particular conception of man profoundly different from the conception of man in an obligations system, especially in the case of the Jewish system of morality.

The function of rights is to protect the individual's freedom of action. Rights thus express the moral value of that freedom. A moral system which made rights paramount would treat freedom of action as man's greatest value. It would see man's essence in his will, and his greatest good in the free exercise of that will. A dictumof Immanuel Kant expresses this idea well: Treat each man as an end in himself, and never as a means. To treat someone else as a means to my ends violates the intrinsic value of his will, as if his will has less value than mine. That can never be true if the free exercise of the will is man's greatest value. Notice that nothing depends upon what the will chooses (except its possible conflict with someone else). The choices to perform lifesaving surgery, write a book, go swimming, or go to sleep are all on a par in this respect. If you want to perform surgery and I want to sleep, you may not force me to help with the operation. That would make me a means to your ends and contradict the value of my will.

These consequences hold only for a system in which rights are paramount. We saw above that our intuitive moral judgments are quite different from this: Rights give way to social welfare. What conception of man this type of system implies depends upon the definition of welfare — what is/are the good/s of society. We also saw that rights play no role in the Jewish moral system. It is based instead upon obligations which have their origin in God's will. What definition of social welfare do these obligations embody? This is a very large question, but briefly we can say this. Ultimately, the function of the will is to bring us into a certain relationship with God — a relationship of love. The obligations imposed upon us by God's will are means to this end. Through them we strengthen our consciousness of God, and develop God-like character traits, to the point where the profound mutuality and empathy required by love can exist. In this context it is still possible to see the will as man's essence. But merely exercising the will freely, *without any consideration of which actions are chosen*, is not the paramount value. The will is a power and a potentiality which achieves its value from the way it is used. Only if it is used to bring man closer to God does the will realize its true potential and achieve absolute value.

Questions & Answers

LEVEL ONE

I don't understand what you have against the right to a free education. Americans certainly do have that right: It is part of our democratically passed laws!

You are correct in terms of *legal* rights. American laws give every child the legal right to a free secondary school education. But my concern is with *moral* rights. Moral rights don't depend upon laws. If Americans democratically changed the education laws and required students to pay, they wouldn't have the legal right to a free education any more. That's why the Declaration of Independence speaks of *inalienable* rights. These are rights which cannot be revoked by a change of legislation. And I am not *against* free education. I only want it to be clear that this involves a claim to society's resources and not a right to non-interference of the kind protected by the Constitution.

Why are you opposed to compulsory education and consumer protection? You said that the government is unjustified in enforcing these things. It seems to me that learning to read and protecting public health are certainly important enough to justify government action.

I am not opposed to compulsory education and consumer protection. And I didn't say that the government's activities in these areas is unjustified. I said that it can't be justified *in terms of rights to non-interference.* In fact, those activities contradict those rights. But they can be justified by appeal to social welfare, and I fully agree with that appeal.

You seem to emphasize property rights in your examples — income tax, unpasteurized milk, the integrated luncheonette, the Tudor castle. Why are these rights so important? They aren't even mentioned in the Declaration of Independence.

First of all, I gave plenty of examples not involving property — compulsory education, school busing, laetril, seat belts and travel to Cuba. Second, property rights are an expression of liberty and pursuit of happiness. If the government can take my property at will, or dictate how I may use it, then my liberty and my right to pursue happiness as I understand it are severely limited.

If I understood you, you said that if I give permission to someone to kill me then his obligation not to kill me is canceled. Of course, you meant this only for a non-religious system of morality. But even for such a system there are surely other considerations — the feelings of relatives, obligations I may have — in fact, all the considerations which apply to suicide apply here as well.

You are quite right that in general many factors are relevant even to killing with permission. I used the example with the contrary-to-fact assumption that the *only* source for the obligation not to kill is the right to live. If that were so, then giving permission would cancel the obligation. The point of making such an assumption was to illustrate the difference between obligations arising solely from rights and other types of obligations.

Questions & Answers

LEVEL TWO

You said that we will sacrifice rights to social welfare. Not everyone agrees to that sacrifice: Libertarians hold that rights really are paramount and that social welfare is not a reason to restrict them.

What you say is true. Libertarians make the free choice of the individual more important than any social value (except perhaps survival). Thus they would disagree with all my examples. But the libertarians are a very small group. Is any of you against consumer protection? Compulsory education? Graduated income tax? My argument is based upon the accepted judgments of almost all members of democratic societies.

You made a comparison between selling pornography and unpasteurized milk. It seems to me there is an important difference between the two. Selling pornography is an exercise of free speech, the communication of ideas and information (much as we deplore those ideas). Selling unpasteurized milk is a matter of property rights. That is not nearly as important as free speech.

I agree with you that different rights are involved in the two cases, and that free speech may be more important than property rights. My point was only this: If we take into consideration *only rights* then *neither* can be restricted. Both involve inalienable rights which are lost, even if they are not the same rights. Someone who defends distributing pornography on the grounds of defending our inalienable right to free speech ought to defend the sale of unpasteurized milk on the grounds of defending our inalienable right to freedom and pursuit of happiness.

I was very surprised by your remark concerning John Stuart Mill. When I read his On Liberty in college, I understood him to be squarely behind rights in principle, and against society's interference with the individual's free choice.

You are not alone, many people understand Mill that way. But there is a problem. Mill wrote another book called *Utilitarianism.* In that book he identifies social utility as the *sole criterion* of all ethical judgment. A right is defined there as an activity concerning which it will benefit society for the government to protect our freedom. So we possess a moral right only when it can be justified by appeal to social welfare. Now you may say that this is merely an inconsistency — perhaps Mill changed his mind. (*On Liberty* was published in 1859, *Utilitarianism* in 1861. This makes a very rapid change of mind on a very profound point.) But Mill reiterates in *On Liberty* itself the primacy of utility: "It is proper to state that I forego any advantage which could be derived to my argument from the idea of abstract right, as a thing independent of utility. I regard utility as the ultimate appeal on all ethical questions. . .." (p.79).[1] There is no conception of an inalienable right in principle, but rather an assessment of the effects on social

1. All page references are to Mill, J.S., *Utilitarianism on Liberty and Considerations on Representative Government,* ed. H.B. Acton, Dent, 1972.

utility of granting rights. Take free speech for example. Mill has four reasons for granting this right (pp.120-1): "First, if any opinion is compelled to silence, that opinion may ... be true. Secondly, ... it may ... contain a portion of the truth. Thirdly, ... unless [the received opinion] is ... vigorously and earnestly contested, it will ... be held in the manner of a prejudice, with little comprehension or feeling of its rational grounds. And ... fourthly, the meaning of the doctrine itself will be in danger of being lost, ... and deprived of its vital effect on the character and conduct ...." Here only utility is at stake: finding the truth, exercising rational judgment and preserving the meaning and effect of true beliefs. Try justifying the right to disseminate pornography on these grounds! Perhaps one more quotation will suffice. "But the strongest of all the arguments against the interference of the public with purely personal conduct is that, when it does interfere, the odds are that it interferes wrongly, and in the wrong place." In other words, the interference is not wrong in principle, but likely to do more harm than good due to ignorance of, or indifference to the true interests of the individual interfered with. Thus Mill explicitly takes the position that rights are only justified by their contribution to social welfare.

You have stressed the conflict between rights and social welfare. Perhaps if rights are understood negatively, as strict non-interference, there is a conflict. But some people feel that this is an unrealistic conception of rights. They argue that the function of rights is to protect freedom. For your negative rights this is obvious; my right not to be interfered with in doing X protects my freedom to do X. But if we analyze freedom we can see that we ought to recognize positive rights as well. Freedom is the ability to choose among alternatives. We can enhance freedom in two different ways: (1) We can prevent coercion, and (2)

*we can provide more alternatives to choose from. The first
is covered by your negative rights, the second by welfare.
But they both have the same purpose, viz. promoting
freedom. In fact, it could be argued that the first without
the second is worth very little. Freedom of movement is not
very significant to a person who is indigent, malnourished
and ill. Freedom of self-expression means little to someone
who is illiterate. By providing a minimum standard of
living we increase freedom by increasing the alternatives
that can be realistically chosen. Thus your negative rights
on the one hand, and welfare on the other, have the same
ultimate rationale — to promote freedom. Why then deny
the title "rights" to the basic human needs stressed by
welfare? In fact, there are those who would mix the terms
and call the obligation to satisfy those needs welfare
rights![2] You probably would regard this as a self-contra-
diction, but why?*

You're right. I do think "welfare rights" is self-contra-
dictory. The reason is relatively simple. It is true that rights
— real, negative rights — and so-called "welfare rights"
both enhance freedom in the way you describe. However,
there is still enough which distinguishes them to make their
ultimate rationale fundamentally different. The basic
difference can be put in terms of how we describe the
violation of these rights. Take a simple pair of cases: (1) I
steal your car, (2) you have no car, ask me to give you one,
and I refuse. Now in both cases I am related to the
restriction of your freedom: because of me you don't have
the option of using a car. But morally the cases are very
different. In case (1) you have been *victimized*, *robbed*,
treated *unjustly*. If government policy is involved, we may
label the government a *tyranny*. In case (2), none of these

---

2. See Gutman, Amy, *Liberal Equality*, Cambridge U. Press, 1980, esp.
pp. 5-12.

descriptions applies. Of course, even in case (2) I might be guilty of *insensitivity*, and I may be *failing to live up to obligations of charity*. But this is a far cry from victimizing, etc. Now it seems to me that the word "rights" is supposed to highlight the differences between these two cases. That is why I oppose describing case (2) as the violation of "welfare rights".

By the way, in your own words, I detect a struggle between these two points of view. You start by saying that the function of rights is to *protect* freedom. This I applaud. But when you shift to speaking of *enhancing or promoting* freedom, that is another matter altogether. Negative rights protect freedom. Enhancing or promoting freedom is the job of a variety of means, including rights and welfare. But just because they share this particular function is no reason not to recognize their other moral differences.

You said that waiver and redress are two key differences between a rights system and a system of obligations like Jewish Law. It seems to me that the distinction is not so absolute. We could put conditions on the obligations which would mimic the way rights function. For example, George might say (to the fellow who promised not to destroy your watch), "But if Gottlieb allows you to destroy it, then I release you from this promise." Surely Jewish Law must incorporate this type of thing into property law. How else could anything be bought or sold if obligations not to interfere couldn't be transferred at will?

I think your point is correct in part. Waiver conditions can be included in obligations. As you say, this is necessary to be able to transfer property. The *destruction* of property is another matter, however. Jewish Law forbids wanton destruction, so that obligation will not be subject to waiver.

And it is not clear that appropriateness of redress is transferable at all. If George says: "If you destroy Gottlieb's watch, I give him permission to redress your failure to keep your promise," does that make it *morally* permissible for me to redress what is really a crime against George? If not, we still have a clear difference between rights and obligations.

However, the real point is not whether obligations could be given special conditions to imitate rights. The point is that *without* such conditions obligations function differently from rights, and these differences imply entirely different foundations. Rights imply that others' obligations to me are due to the intrinsic importance of my will. Therefore those obligations are under my control of waiver and redress. Obligations which do not stem from rights imply the importance of their source. Only if He dictates conditions of waiver and redress will they really apply.

The
Chosen
People

I. *Equality*

A. Descriptive

1. Obviously true in some respects — birth, death, some aspects of happiness
2. Obviously untrue in some respects — intelligence, character (even as related to moral action), some aspects of happiness
3. Equality from birth is unproven, irrelevant
4. Similarly for nations — differences in "national character"
5. Conflict with chosenness only if chosenness violates clear descriptive equalities (it does not)

B. Prescriptive — rights and responsibilities

1. Principled exceptions — draft law, education for disadvantaged, right to vote
2. Prescriptive equality except for morally relevant differences — *equality* becomes irrelevant
3. Rights and responsibilities really distributed
4. Conflict with chosenness only if chosenness violates those specific characteristics (it does not)
5. Cf. Peter Weston, "The Empty Idea of Equality," *Harvard Law Review*, 1982 and subsequent discussion in Yale, Michigan and Georgia Law Reviews

C. Ideal=to *create* (approximate) equality

1. Differential treatment in order to lessen functional inequalities (e.g., handicapped)
2. No conflict with chosenness

D. Racism — conversion, matriarchal descent

II. The Chosen People

A. Chosenness with respect to task *only*

    1. Inconsistent with classical sources — cf. *Pirkei Avos* III:18; *Kuzari I, passim; Derech Hashem* II:4 "How odd of God . . ." — given difference of national character choice cannot be arbitrary

B. Spiritual difference partly "inherited," partly historical

    1. Egyptian exile, exodus, Sinai revelation, wilderness experience, conquest of Israel

C. Spiritual difference must fit *detailed* legal and religious differences

    1. General description of Jewish task (and nature) — to exemplify ultimate non-comparative value

        a. Non-comparative value *justifies existence*

        b. Moral — spiritual quality of *tzaddik*-like moments possess non-comparative value

◄§ Equality

THE IDEA OF CHOSENNESS IS RECEIVED NEGA-
tively nowadays. the political and intellectual climate is
against it. The great passion of our time is equality —
equal rights and responsibilities for all, based upon our
shared humanity. Chosenness seems to set one group apart from the
rest of mankind as superior, and therefore possessing special
privileges and advantages. This strikes the modern mind as false
and unfair — and quite possibly racist. With this type of initial
reaction, even normally open minds tend to close. Any discussion
of what chosenness means is then lost in a storm of negative
emotions.

For this reason I have found it useful to start with a discussion of equality. When we appreciate the differences among various concepts of equality, and the limitations of our commitments to each, we will be more open minded in our examination of the traditional concept of Jewish chosenness. Three different concepts of equality will be considered: *Descriptive* equality (people are *in fact* equal), *prescriptive* equality (people *should be treated* equally), and *ideal* equality (people *should be made* as equal as possible). The extent of our commitment to each will be explored, together with the possibility of conflict with chosenness. We will then be able to turn to a discussion of the idea of chosenness itself.

(1) *Descriptive equality:* "We hold these truths to be self-evident, that all men are created equal..." The Declaration of Independence thus states its belief that people *are in fact equal* to one another. (Indeed, it holds this belief to be *self-evident* — not requiring any investigation, evidence, argument, etc.!) Now in some respects this is clearly true. We are all born (at least, until cloning is perfected), we all die, we all breathe, eat, sleep, excrete, etc. Certain experiences affect us with pleasure (love, success, ice cream) and pain (failure, a visit to the dentist). But in other respects it is clearly false. We vary considerably in physical characteristics (height, weight, strength, coordination, color, beauty), intelligence, personality traits (sympathy, sensitivity, industry, self-control) and certain sources of pleasure (Bach is preferred by some, the Beatles by others). Given all these differences, does a blanket assertion of equality make any sense? The truth is that we are all equal in some respects and unequal in others. Since we cannot say that the former are more numerous (how would we count respects?) or more important (are breathing and nutrition more important than intelligence and character?), assertations of blanket equality serve only to divert attention from the differences.

Some respond to these observations by saying that the differences cited hold only for adults and are the result of family, education and culture. As babies, we are all equal, and if we equalized opportunity, we would be more equal as adults. Now even if this were true, it is not clear what it proves. We *do* differ as adults, and it is impossible to equalize all aspects of environmental influence (not all children can be the oldest in the family; parents will differ in their abilities; climates and natural resources will vary, etc., etc.). Thus adult differences are a permanent feature of humanity. Furthermore, the belief in baby equality is based upon no direct evidence (we cannot test the intelligence and character of newborns directly). Babies certainly differ in some respects, as various birth defects and genetic syndromes show. The extent of their differences simply cannot be measured at the present time. The belief in baby equality thus lacks evidence and is of doubtful relevance.

It should be pointed out that just as individuals differ in character and abilities, so do nations. They are consistently strong in certain areas and weak in others. The United States, for example, is consistently strong in technology and weak in fundamental theoretical science.(No United States scientist has made a theoretical contribution on a par with Newton, Maxwell, Rutherford, Bohr, Planck, Einstein, Heisenberg, etc. — work that will be read with interest a hundred years later. Michaelson and Marley, who devised the experiment which prepared the way for [simple] relativity, failed to understand its theoretical implications and judged it a failure.) Germanic education has produced one-third of the Nobel prizes in science in this century. The intellectual-cultural contribution of the Jewish people throughout the millennia, and especially in the last century, is vastly out of proportion to their numbers and objective opportunities. And there are differences of accepted practices as well. Much of the British police force goes without firearms; in the United States that would be unthinkable. The explanation of these differences is problematic, just as it is for individuals. Whether they are wholly the effect of environment and experience, or in part reflect inherent differences, is impossible to prove at present.

How does descriptive equality, to the extent that it is true, affect Jewish chosenness? If Judaism asserts that Jews and non-Jews differ across the board in some respect, and we could *prove* that (some) Jews and non-Jews are equal *in that respect*, then chosenness would be unacceptable. What we cannot do is oppose chosenness by a blind, blanket commitment to equality: "You say Jews are different? We believe that all people are equal so you must be wrong." When we examine the respects in which Judaism distinguishes Jews from non-Jews, we will see that none of them are subject to objective disproof. Thus Judaism has no difficulty with descriptive equality.

(2) *Prescriptive equality:* The equal assignment of rights and responsibilities to all citizens is often taken as the hallmark of a democratic society. Singling out a particular group for special rights and responsibilities seems to undermine equality of all citizens before the law. But is it really true that democracy requires no legal distinctions between citizens? Let's consider some examples.

Until recently the United States draft law could be written roughly as follows: A citizen age eighteen shall be subject to the draft unless the citizen is female, a college student, has an I.Q. under 60, is a paraplegic, part of a family of which two members have died in foreign wars of the United States, etc. This law assigns an awesome responsibility: to risk one's life in defense of the nation. Is this responsibility applied equally to all citizens? It seems not, since those under eighteen years of age, female, studying in college, etc., are exempted.

As a second example, consider education. We expect that the right to free, public schooling should be equal for all citizens. But is it? Blind, deaf, crippled and other handicapped children receive many times more the funds allotted to the education of normal children. Equal right to education ought to mean that the same amount of money should be spent on each student; if the children of a particular religious group or political party received extra funds, we would surely call that undemocratic discrimination. But as the examples of handicapped children show, no one believes in equal allotments for *all* students. The same holds for many other social services: welfare only for the indigent, medicare only for the elderly, etc.

Finally, let's examine the most characteristic right of democratic societies — the right to vote. Is voting equal for all citizens? There are restrictions of age, citizenship, residence (if you live in New Jersey, you can't vote in New York even if you work in Manhattan and have great interest in New York's laws) and criminal conviction. Even voting is assigned to a specific group and not granted blindly to all.

What these examples show is that we *do* single out groups of citizens for special privileges and responsibilities. Now it is sometimes objected that these distinctions are the result of democratic legal procedures and therefore reflect "the will of the people." "If that is the way the society wants to distribute rights and responsibilities, it is its prerogative to do so." Now perhaps it is correct that societies have this authority to distinguish among their citizens (though the example of the Nazis remind us that there are limits). However, the objection misses the point: These social decisions show that societies are not committed to treating their citizens *equally*. To legitimize their ability to make distinctions among their citizens is to *support* our observation that those distinctions are acceptable.

A second common response is that no one expects equality to be *blind* (even though, in classical statuary, that is the way justice is usually represented!). Of course relevant differences must be taken into account in assigning rights and responsibilities. There is no point in assigning a cripple to the infantry, or in allowing ten-year-olds to vote. Surely what equality means is that *people who have all the same relevant characteristics should be treated the same*. With this objection I think we can agree. It concedes that distinctions be made among citizens on the basis of relevant characteristics, and only when people do not differ in these respects are they to be treated the same. But then *equality* can be completely dispensed with in describing rights and responsibilities. To be told, "All and only male, eighteen-year-old, physically and mentally fit non-college students, etc., are eligible for the draft," is to be told who is and who is not eligible. To add, "All those (non-)eligible are *equally* (non-)eligible," does nothing to the rule at all. Thus in practice, associated with each right or responsibility will be a description of the group of people to which it applies. To be told that people are still being treated equally since everyone, *if* under eighteen, female, etc., also *would be* exempt from the draft, does not equalize rights and responsibilities in the *real* world. One might as well have told American women before 1920 that they had equal voting rights since *if* they were men, they *would* be able to vote!

How does this conclusion relate to Jewish chosenness? If it could be demonstrated that a right or responsibility which morally ought to apply to a particular group were assigned by Judaism to a different group, then there would be an objection against Judaism. The case would have to be argued *in specifics*. It cannot be asserted: "We are against distinctions in rights and responsibilities *in principle* and *therefore* cannot tolerate any idea of chosenness." As we have seen, no one holds such a principle of equality.

(3). *Ideal equality:* This idea takes for granted that people *are* different, and should be treated differently. It asserts that one *goal* of this treatment ought to be the reduction of differences between people, insofar as this is possible. The extra money spent on educating the handicapped is an excellent example. The point of singling them out for special (unequal) treatment is to help them become as independent and functional as possible. Thus they will become as much like the normal population as possible. This is an ideal with which Judaism can wholly agree. Chosenness in no way opposes efforts to reduce differences, when those efforts take realistic account of the inherent limitations the differences impose.

In sum, there is no obvious conflict between equality and the Jewish idea of chosenness. The case for a conflict would have to be made by finding specific descriptive or prescriptive Jewish distinctions which can be conclusively refuted. It cannot be made by mouthing slogans of blanket equality which no one really believes. Concerning the charge of racism, two facts serve to rule it out in any literal sense. The first is conversion — one can voluntarily become Jewish, whereas racial identity cannot be changed. The second is that hereditary Jewishness is *matriarchal* — a person is born a Jew if and only if his mother is Jewish. The identity of the father is irrelevant. No racial identification can depend only upon a person's mother. Of course, one may admit that Jews are not a race and yet object to *any* group being described and treated differently. But then, as we have just seen, the burden will be upon him to argue his case in detail.

⊷§ Chosenness

A full account of the Jewish idea of chosenness would require answering such questions as: In what ways — descriptive and prescriptive — does Judaism distinguish between Jews and non-Jews? Are these differences inherent? If so, how is conversion possible? How did these differences come about? Why are they dependent only upon maternal ancestry?

In order to hold our discussion to manageable size, we will focus on one general characterization of chosenness. But first, we need to clear away a popular misconception.

There is a widespread understanding of chosenness which restricts this idea to task only. Jews are not inherently different from other people; they have a unique *challenge* to live a certain way of life which may inspire others. God has a moral-spiritual message which is to be delivered to mankind via the living example of the Jewish people. But, in principle, many other nations could have been chosen for this purpose.

As convenient as this understanding is from an egalitarian point of view, it is unacceptable for two reasons. First, it is incompatible with the classical Jewish sources on the subject. (See *Derech Hashem*, II:4 and the sources cited there.) Therefore it cannot be an account of the classical Jewish concept. Second, it gives an extremely peculiar picture of God's process of choice. We noted above that nations differ in character. These differences will affect a nation's appropriateness for so comprehensive a challenge as the total Jewish way of life. That challenge emphasizes certain traits of character: humility, self-sacrifice, courage, steadfastness, etc. It demands the development of certain abilities: deep human understanding, intellectualism and scholarship, and a philosophical understanding of life. It requires enormous behavioral self-discipline to respond to each life situation in accordance with a detailed, idealized plan of action. To think that the differences between nations will not substantially affect their appropriateness for this challenge is patently unreasonable. The choice could not have been arbitrary: God must have chosen the Jewish people for this challenge because their abilities and propensities made them the most appropriate for it.

Of course, even if we agree that there is a unique fit between Jewish national character and the Torah way of life, this does not explain how that character was formed. Concerning national character in general, opinions divide on the relative contributions of historical experience and inherent endowments. This debate parallels the discussion of baby equality, and is similarly impossible to resolve objectively in our present state of knowledge. Therefore we may note the account in Jewish sources without fear of objective refutation. Briefly, Jewish national character is the result of both factors mentioned above: Certain basic traits are inherited from the patriarchs, and then molded by historical experience. The patriarchs, due to the inherent quality of their souls and their enormous self-development, established the foundations of Jewish character. This foundation is then the starting point for all future Jewish experience. (Although it is "passed down" from generation to generation, we must not think of it in genetic terms. Remember that only maternal ancestry counts, and it is available to converts. This is a *spiritual* transmission.) After all, objective circumstances do not determine the content of experience: One person may be exhilarated by a challenge while a second may be totally unnerved. Slavery in Egypt, the exodus, the revelation at Sinai, the forty years in the wilderness, the conquest of the land of Israel — as experienced by the fundamental patriarchal character — produced the basis of Jewish national character.

What can be said specifically about this unique character of the Jewish people? Of course, using the correspondence between challenge and ability, we could survey the entire corpus of Jewish law and values and then say: The uniqueness of the Jew is that his inherent nature is appropriate for *this* challenge. But this is utterly impractical since it would take several lifetimes to complete the survey. Instead, let's try to get some general perspective on the challenge, and use that as an indicator of a general description of Jewish uniqueness.

There is an important, little-known distinction concerning value. (The idea, and its application to chosenness, were brought to my attention by Rabbi Nochum Lansky.) Some things are valuable because they are better than the alternative. They have, we might say, *comparative value*; they are preferable in comparison with what will happen if they are not realized. For example, health is preferable to disease, education to ignorance, and being loved to being hated. By contrast, some things are valuable without consideration of any alternatives or comparisons. We might call this *non-comparative value*. This type of value is difficult to explain. Whenever we consider the value of a thing, aren't we at least implicitly comparing it with its alternative? If we consider the value of health, can we ignore the fact that the alternative is disease and that health is preferable to disease?

I think we can. Let's consider two illustrations. Imagine God deciding whether to create the universe. He asks your opinion. (Don't ask me how *you* got here!) If you can answer, "Yes — create the universe so that X will come into existence, because X is valuable," then you are judging that X has non-comparative value. For, as things stand now, *neither X nor its alternative exist.* Thus recommending X in these circumstances cannot be the result of comparison with an alternative. As a second illustration, imagine a prediction of mankind's imminent demise (the earth is to pass through deadly radiation). You describe this as an immense tragedy. When asked why, you answer, "Because without mankind X will disappear, and X is valuable." Here again, your judgment accords X non-comparative value. For, when mankind disappears neither X nor its alternative will exist. Thus to say health has non-comparative value means that health could be a reason for creating the universe: "Create mankind," we might say, "since some people will be healthy, and health is valuable." Or: "Mankind's disappearance is a tragedy since there will be no more health." These judgments don't depend upon health being preferable to disease.

The crucial difference between the two types of value is this: Comparative value relates to a *particular state* of a thing, while non-comparative value relates to its *very existence.* If health is merely preferable to disease, then being healthy is a valuable state of an already existing person, but it is no reason to create another person. Something which has non-comparative value makes the existence of its possessor valuable. We now arrive at the central question: *What has non-comparative value?*

I think we can rule out certain candidates immediately. Wealth might be preferable to poverty, but it could hardly be a reason for creating the universe. Health is preferable to disease, but the loss of healthy specimens is not a reason to mourn mankind's passing. Education is preferable to ignorance, but the mere possession of information does not make our very existence valuable. The same could be said of many common values — fame, power, intelligence, etc. What then is left which really does have non-comparative value?

Classical Judaism has an answer to this question, however here we run into a fundamental problem. It is really impossible to put the answer into words — it has to be experienced to be understood. Nevertheless, I will try to say something. It is a certain moral-spiritual quality of life which in Jewish terms has non-comparative value. A person who achieves this quality sufficiently throughout his life is called a *tzaddik*. The rest of us achieve this value during intermittent moments of striving to become more like a *tzaddik*. If we had to advise God on creating the universe, or mourn mankind's passing, our reason would be that some people will be *tzaddikim*, and others will strive to become *tzaddikim*. For the sake of that value it is worthwhile for the universe to exist, and mankind's demise would be an immeasurable tragedy. Now since it is a quality of life which is in question, it must at least be observed (if not experienced) in order to be understood. But perhaps a few incidents from the lives of *tzaddikim* will give a hint at its nature.

R. Moshe Feinstein arrived one morning at his yeshiva. As he got out of the car, the driver unwittingly slammed the door on his fingers. R. Moshe hid his stricken hand and, biting his lips with pain, walked into the building without giving any visible sign to the driver. When those who observed the incident asked his reason for acting thus, he explained: "That young man was so generous to drive me to the yeshiva. Could I hurt his feelings by showing him that something went wrong?" Now remember that Judaism is not a religion of self-torture — we do not lie on beds of nails, etc. — R. Moshe *did feel* the pain. Furthermore, he was not prepared for it. (On the way to the dentist you stir up your courage in order to bear the pain quietly.) The impact of the door on his fingers triggered two contradictory impulses — a cry of pain and a desire not to embarrass the driver. The latter won out because R. Moshe's involvement with another person's embarrassment was deeper and more powerful than response to his own physical pain! This is an indication of the unique moral level that Judaism requires.

Two incidents from the beginning of this century illustrate the intensity of Jewish spirituality. The Modzitzer Rebbe had a leg amputated. No anesthesia was available. During the operation he composed a 64-part musical composition. R. Naftali Amsterdam required an operation and *refused* anesthesia on the grounds that he did not want his Talmudic research interrupted! These men possessed the ability to focus on the spiritual to the point that physical awareness and sensation were completely blocked out. (I am not appealing to the supernatural here. We all experience this to some degree: focusing on one aspect of our experience partly blocks awareness of other aspects. For example, athletes often feel the full intensity of the pain only after the competition is over. What isunique in Jewish spirituality is the *degree* of focus, and its object — involvement with God.)

These events illustrate a total absorption in the moral-spiritual dimension of life. It is this quality of experience and action which Judaism accords non-comparative value. For a greater appreciation I recommend the biographies of R. Aryeh Levin (*A Tzaddik in Our Time*) and R. Moshe Feinstein (*Reb Moshe*). In the meantime, we can say this. The whole of Jewish Law and values is designed to develop this quality of life. If, as we said above, Jewish national character is uniquely suited to this challenge, then we can describe what makes the Jew different as follows. The Jew is naturally suited to developing the moral-spiritual dimension of life to the point where it determines his experience and action. *This* is his chosenness.

Questions & Answers

LEVEL ONE

You said at the beginning that people object to chosenness because it implies that Jews are better than other people. I don't see that you have answered this. If anything, your description of moral-spiritual uniqueness makes it worse!

Well, I hoped to weaken the complaint somewhat by pointing out that people do differ, even with respect to moral characteristics like sympathy or anger. Thus Jewish uniqueness cannot be opposed in the name of universal moral equality. But there is a deeper problem here. Let's distinguish between *better performance* on the one hand, and *deserving more credit* on the other. The two are independent of one another. A gifted person may achieve excellent performance easily and deserve little credit, a person with average capabilities may achieve quite good performance through enormous effort, thus deserving much credit. Now it seems to me an objective fact that in terms of moral-spiritual *performance*, the traditional Jewish community is, and has been, outstanding. This can be established via statistics of violent crime, drug addiction, divorce, literacy, etc. The question of *credit*, however, is much more complicated. Credit depends upon the natural gifts one brings to the task. This evaluation can be made by no one except God. The characteristics inherited from the patriarchs, together with our Divinely guided national history, represent our "natural" gifts. They are so different from the natural gifts of other nations that it is impossible for us to assess relative merit.

You gave examples of national character, including characteristics of the United States. But Americans are mostly immigrants coming from many different nations. How can they have a single national character?

That is an interesting point. Nevertheless, if the consistent differences I cited are correct, then national character is a reality, in spite of America's immigrant history. Your observation will be important for *explaining* how national character is *formed*. Perhaps the mix of nationalities under frontier conditions had a strong effect.

But then how can you say that there is some fixed, given national character if you allow that mixing and environmental conditions help create it?

I didn't say that national character is *fixed*. On the contrary, I said explicitly that our "natural" gifts include our national history. However, I did point out that *how* history is *experienced* — what effect historical conditions have on the development of national character — depends upon the national character brought to the experience. Two nations may be impoverished and derive opposite commitments from that condition: the one to practice charity, and the other to achieve wealth. Thus original, *given* (but not *fixed*) national character will have a continuing effect on future development.

Questions & Answers

LEVEL TWO

Your discussion of prescriptive equality came to the conclusion that this nation plays no role in assigning rights or responsibilities. Now I agree that we do make exceptions and treat people differently when they have morally relevant differences — we don't send a cripple to the infantry. But it seems to me that equality is still a starting point — in the absence of proof of difference we ought to treat people equally.

So your motto is: "Equal until proven different." But I think that even this is a mistake. (Here I follow Peter Weston, "The Empty Idea of Equality," *Harvard Law Review*, 1982.) Which is worse — to treat really equal people unequally (e.g., to put one able-bodied man in the infantry and another in a safe desk job), or to treat really unequal people equally (e.g., to put a handicapped person in the infantry along with physically normal people)? Isn't it obvious that we cannot say as a rule which is worse? If so, the only honest thing to do is to suspend the decision until we have better information. In the case of the infantry this will mean not assigning the person until we know that he is equal!

You say that Jews possess a natural moral-spiritual superiority, partly as an inheritance from the patriarchs,

and partly as a result of unique historical experiences.
Well, if you mean that all Jews and no non-Jews possess
this characteristic, your assertion strikes me as outrageous.
I know Jews who are perfect scoundrels, and non-Jews
who behave in an exemplary manner, and surely you do as
well. I refuse to believe that Judaism would assert
something so obviously false, and even bigoted!

I hope that the obviously strong feelings you have on
this subject will not prevent you from *thinking* about it.
The moral-spiritual uniqueness of each and every Jew is a
potentiality, not a finished product. You cannot prove that
a potentiality does not exist by citing cases in which it is not
manifest; they may be cases of arrested development.
(Human infants growing up among animals will not speak,
even though they obviously had the ability to *learn* to
speak when born.) Similarly, you cannot prove that a
specific potentiality exists without very careful controlled
experiment action. (A color-blind person will learn eventually that grass is green, the top traffic light is red, etc., so
that to a casual observer his sight may seem normal.) Thus
the mere fact that some Jews misbehave and some
non-Jews are exemplary does not disprove my statement.
To say that Jews have this special potentiality is to say that
under certain specific conditions Jews and non-Jews will
develop differently. As far as external conditions are
concerned — economics, population size and density,
political status, etc. — we can make reasonable comparisons. But cultural input will usually be very different, so it
is very difficult to imagine a conclusive test. The traditional
position is therefore not refuted by your observations.

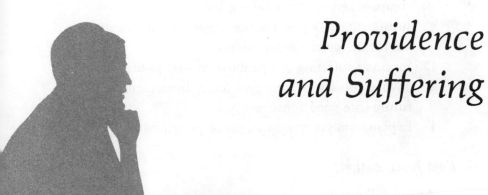

Providence
and Suffering

I. General Principles

A. Objector must show omniscience, omnipotence, and justice imply suffering is impossible

B. General explanation, not for individual cases — compare physics for a falling leaf

C. Justification via past (justice, desert) vs. justification via future (good consequences)

D. Innocent suffering is a problem of past justification

E. Two approaches — via past (deny innocence) or via future (cite good consequences)

F. Explanation via combinations of principles

II. Past Justification

A. "Good" people
   1. Possibility of bad private life
   2. Incomplete list of responsibilities
   3. Higher standard

B. Self-inflicted suffering

C. Reincarnation (*gilgul neshamos*)

D. Past justification alone would be sufficient

III. Future justification

A. Cosmic — free will requires no obvious Divine intervention, so no systematic prevention or punishment of evil, hence innocents will suffer

B. Social
   1. Clarify motivation of righteous to set example
   2. To atone for generation

C. Personal
   1. Suffering to focus on essential life agenda against temptation
   2. Develop moral capacities

3. Eliminate failures in this world
4. Increase reward in *Olam Haba* (savage — gems)

IV. *Absolute contradiction only if proven that none of the justifications applies — clearly impossible; goodness and mercy modify strict justice*

✥ General Principles

WHY DO THE INNOCENT SUFFER? THE question is thousands of years old. Jewish sources, from the earliest to the latest, address themselves to it. It occurs to every thinking person with an interest in religion. We all know cases of good people who suffer terrible agonies for no obvious reason. From a religious perspective this disturbs us because it seems to contradict certain basic Jewish beliefs. In particular, we believe: (1) God is omniscient (He knows everything); (2) God is omnipotent (He can do anything); (3) God is just. If these beliefs are correct, how is it possible that innocent people suffer? If God is omniscient, then He *knows* about their suffering. If He is omnipotent, then He *could* prevent or relieve it.

If He is just, then He *ought* to prevent or relieve it. Since the innocent suffer, it seems that at least one of the above statements must not be true. This is the problem of evil: *The obvious fact of undeserved suffering seems to prove that at least one basic Jewish belief is false.*

The Jewish sources respond to this problem by offering a variety of explanations for suffering. Each explanation does one of two things. a) It may show that what appears to be innocent suffering really is not: The person may be guilty of crimes which make his suffering quite just. This type of explanation denies the "obvious fact" of undeserved suffering in the cases to which it applies. b) It may appeal to the fact that, although God is just, He is not *only* just. Other *moral* considerations like mercy and goodness may outweigh justice in particular cases. This type of explanation solves the contradiction between (1) — (3) and undeserved suffering by rejecting (3) as too *narrow*. A more complete description of God's moral attributes allows the possibility of suffering which justice alone could not allow.

Before we survey some of those explanations, we need to take account of two methodological points. First: The Jewish explanation of suffering will be *general* and *not specific*. In order to understand the difference between general and specific explanations, consider this example. Ask a physicist why, when a leaf falls from a tree, it lands where it does, and he can produce a complete list of relevant factors. The force of gravity, motion of the air, mass and aerodynamic properties of the leaf, etc., together determine the leaf's downward path. Now suppose there is a leaf still attached to the tree, and we ask the physicist to mark the exact spot on the ground where it will land when it falls ten seconds from now. He cannot do it. Does this show that his explanation of why the leaf falls (gravity, air motion, etc. is wrong)? Not at all — he has cited all the relevant factors, but he cannot *quantify* them in a particular case. He cannot ascertain the exact motion of all the molecules of air in the vicinity, the exact aerodynamic characteristics of the leaf and so on. His explanation applies to leaves *generally*, but cannot be applied in detail to any specific leaf. Similarly, the Jewish explanations of suffering will apply generally, but will not be able to explain in detail particular cases of suffering. We will examine twelve different principles, each of which explains some type of suffering. Together they can explain any realistic case of suffering we could imagine. But if asked about a particular person or community, or a particular historical event, we will not be able to say in detail which principles are relevant to what degree. This inability does not invalidate our general explanation any more than the physicist's inability to predict the exact landing point of the leaf invalidates his explanation of why the leaf falls.

The second methodological point is this. There are two different ways in which an action can be justified — via the past or via the future. These types of justification are independent of one another, and may even conflict. For example, suppose you sign a contract with a worker agreeing to pay him $200 for a week's labor. On Friday afternoon he presents himself with his supervisor's positive evaluation. He has fulfilled his part of the contract; you are now obligated to fulfill yours and pay him. To withhold his pay would be unjustified. These judgments appeal only to the *past*. Given the contract you signed and his work, the wages must be paid. By contrast, suppose a stranger requests $200 for an operation. You may regard this as an obligation of charity and feel that you ought to give him the money. To refuse would be unjustified, given his need and your economic resources. Here the considerations are all *future* — the medical difference the money will make to him (in comparison to what the money could do for you). The past is irrelevant. You don't *owe* him money, he has not *earned* it. Only the *future use* of the money justifies the gift.

To see how past justification and future justification may conflict, let's go back to your worker. As you are making out his check, you get a telephone call from his social worker. She tells you that he is planning to use the money to buy a gun to shoot his wife and urges you not to pay him. "I know you signed a contract," she says, "but you will be aiding him in a terrible crime if you pay him." You now have a dilemma. In terms of the past you owe him the money and it is wrong to withhold it. In terms of the future it is wrong to help him commit murder. So the conflict between past and future justification is clear. And if you should decide not to pay him, you are weighing future considerations more heavily than past consideration.

Now let's analyze the problem of evil in terms of the two types of justification. What is the problem *about* — past or future justification? The answer is *past*. The problem concerns *innocent* people suffering. Innocence refers to the *past*: Up until the time of suffering he is blameless and *therefore* his suffering seems unjustified. Since the problem concerns past justification, there are two different ways to approach it. (1) We can deal with it on its own terms and try to justify suffering by appeal to the past. This will mean denying the innocence of the sufferer; contrary to appearances, perhaps he deserves to suffer. In such cases the problem is solved by denying the "obvious fact" of undeserved suffering. (2) We can expand our view to take account of future considerations as well. This means we *admit* that some innocent people suffer, but we take account of the positive good that suffering produces and argue that *the good outweighs the evil.* On balance, then, the suffering is justified *even though the sufferer is innocent.*

Jewish sources apply both approaches. Some explanations show that the supposedly innocent sufferer really deserves his suffering. Others show that the suffering is instrumental in creating some future good. The goal is to *justify the suffering by a combination of the explanations.* By "combination" I mean two things. (1) No one explanation alone is expected to cover all cases of suffering. (2) Some cases may be justified only by applying *several explanations together.* In general terms, it may be that the sufferer is not *so* innocent as we thought, and therefore deserves some portion of his suffering; the rest of his suffering, which is undeserved in terms of the past, is justified by the good it serves to create. If we take into account the fact that explanations may apply to different cases *in different degrees* we see that even a few particular explanations can generate a great variety of justifications for suffering. *To solve the problem of evil we need to find enough particular explanations so that for any case of suffering, some combination of explanations could justify it.* We shall see that Jewish sources do indeed solve the problem of evil.

ᴇᴄ§ Past Justification

We often see someone suffering and ask: "Why him? He is such a kind, considerate person, etc. — surely he doesn't deserve to suffer like that!" Our surprise depends upon our evaluation of his innocence. That evaluation can be questioned in a variety of ways.

(1) How well do we know the sufferer? Perhaps there is a darker side to his life of which we are unaware. A woman once approached me with a horrifying tale of abuse at the hands of her husband. When I suggested she try to apply community pressure through the local rabbi, she answered: "You don't understand. The minute he walks out the front door he is a different person. To the community he is warm, friendly, generous — a model neighbor. Only I know the evil of which he is capable." Now imagine some misfortune strikes her husband. The community will be dismayed even though the suffering is deserved. This case illustrates the first principle of past justification: *The suffering is deserved due to unknown facts of the sufferer's life.*

(2) How do we judge that a person does not deserve to suffer? "He is a good husband and father, he pays his taxes, he volunteers for community projects. . ." The list may go on as long as you like — at the end we have to conclude that *it is enough.* In order to

draw that conclusion we need to know that we have taken account of *all human responsibilities.* If we have omitted some from consideration, our judgment is incompetent. The Talmud[1] recounts that certain people at the fall of the first Temple were marked for destruction. To the objection that these people were righteous, the Talmud answers that in terms of their *individual* responsibilities they were indeed exemplary, but they did not make sufficient effort to try to improve their neighbors. In other words, if we ignore this particular aspect of social responsibility then we must judge them undeserving of suffering. Thus any judgment that suffering is undeserved presupposes that we have not left some human responsibility out of consideration. This gives us the second principle of past justification: *The suffering is deserved due to the sufferer's failure with respect to human responsibilities of which we have failed to take account.*

(3) Even if we assume that we know the sufferer's life in all detail and that our list of human responsibilities is complete, our judgment that he does not deserve to suffer is still open to question. When we say that he does not deserve to suffer — that he is innocent — what do we mean? *Perfectly* innocent? If only the perfectly innocent do not deserve to suffer, then the problem of evil has a very simple solution: Almost no one is *perfectly* innocent! In fact the problem is much broader than that. Often we judge that even though a person is not perfectly innocent, the *amount of guilt he has does not justify his amount of suffering.* In other words, we make a *comparative* judgment: *His suffering is out of proportion to his guilt.* How is this judgment made? When we compare his life to our list of responsibilities we do not require a perfect score. All that is required is a score so high that his suffering is too much. How high a score is that? How can we determine the amount of suffering appropriate to any given state of partial innocence? The Jewish sources regard this question as

---

1. Bab. Talmud, *Shabbos* 55a.

unanswerable. For, God judges a person in terms of his innate capacities and life circumstances. An action which is accounted for Moses a great failure would be for us a trivial mistake. "God is exacting with His close ones to a hair's breadth!"[2] Now even if we can evaluate a person's *performance* vis-a-vis human responsibilities *in general*, we cannot know in detail what resources he brought to the task. I cannot know in detail your personal strengths and weaknesses, the extent to which you must struggle to accomplish moral and spiritual goals. So I have no way of knowing whether your accomplishment represents a heroic effort and deserves great credit, or is far less then you could have achieved. This gives us the third principle of past justification: *The suffering is deserved because the sufferer is being judged by a higher standard due to his greater abilities.*

(4) Another important type of past justification considers *self-induced suffering.*[3] A great many of our illnesses and accidents are caused by distorted values and lack of self-control. How much heart disease, not to mention mental illness, results from pursuing unnecessary luxuries? Smoking, excess drinking, poor diet, lack of exercise, etc., take an enormous physical toll; anger, pride, jealousy and other undesirable character traits createtremendous emotional strain (which has its own physical consequences). A significant portion of our resources — both physical and human — are wasted on war, degrading "entertainment," inter-personal and inter-social competition, and trivial pursuits, instead of improving the quality of life. It is obviously not appropriate to blame God for suffering which is caused by any of these or other similarly irresponsible actions.

(5) The final principle of past justification is reincarnation: Even though his actions in this life do not justify his suffering, *it*

---

2. Bab. Talmud, *Yevomos* 121b.

3. Maimonides, *The Guide of the Perplexed*, III:12; *Beis Elokim, Shaar HaTeshuvah*, chap. 9.

is justified when his actions in his previous life (or lives) are taken into account. It comes as a surprise to many that reincarnation is a Jewish belief. Nevertheless it is there in the sources,[4] and is obviously relevant to the problem of evil.

How do these principles of past justification affect the problem of evil? Strictly speaking, *they would be sufficient to solve the problem by themselves.* Given any case of suffering it could always be argued that the suffering is deserved due to unknown aspects of the sufferer's life, responsibilities which we failed to take into consideration, a higher standard of judgment, his own irresponsible behavior, and/or reincarnation. We could not know in any case that none of these principles applies. (Even the difficult cases of children suffering is covered by the fifth principle.) Thus we could simply deny the "obvious fact" of undeserved suffering and solve the problem in its own terms. But many Jewish sources do not stop here, and so we turn to the second approach to the problem.

✑ Future Justification

We are now going to examine principles which help justify suffering — even when it is undeserved — by considering the good which such suffering creates.

(6) This physical world is designed so that man should have free will.[5] It is free will that makes man more than a puppet (or robot) — that makes his actions and his life significant and meaningful, especially in moral terms. In addition, free will exercised in morally significant situations enables man to *earn* his ultimate reward, and that makes the reward greater in a certain

---

4. Winkler, *The Soul of the Matter* (New York: 1982) chap. I.
5. Luzzato, *The Way of God* (New York: 1977), I:2.

crucial respect. For these reasons (among others), free will and its consequences are regarded as overwhelmingly valuable. Now let's examine the *presuppositions* of free will.

Imagine that Peter hates Paul and wants to do away with him. Peter climbs to his roof holding a high-powered rifle with a telescopic sight and locates Paul in the cross hairs. However, as he pulls the trigger a breeze springs up and blows the bullet astray. When he tries again, a muscle spasm pulls the rifle off target. A third attempt causes the rifle to jam. Eventually Peter gives up trying to shoot Paul and decides to poison his milk instead. But his wife feeds the milk to their cat. Finally when Peter plants a bomb on Paul's car, his car is stolen and the bomb explodes harmlessly in a forest. How long will it take for Peter to realize that there is something that will not let Paul die?

Now imagine Peter's experience expanded to include every attempt to inflict undeserved pain on another — every such attempt is frustrated by some unforeseen power — how long will it take mankind to realize that causing others undeserved pain is impossible? And once it is seen to be impossible it is no longer a serious alternative for our free will. There is no need to will not to fly, or to will not to push over skyscrapers barehanded! Similarly, once we realized the impossibility of causing undeserved pain, there would be no need to will not to do so. We would not have a realistic alternative of choosing this kind of evil, and so our choices *between* good and evil would be psychologically predetermined. Thus the great majority of decisions between social good and evil would no longer be subject to our free will. This, as we noted above, would compromise the value of this world.

Let's return to Peter on his roof and imagine a slightly different scenario. This time the first bullet flies true and Paul is mortally wounded, but Peter is immediately struck by lightning! If Peter steals a newspaper, a passerby's cigarette ash sends it up in flames, etc. In other words, Peter is successful in his evil plans, but is immediately punished. Now imagine these experiences as universal laws: Every attempt to inflict undeserved suffering is immediately punished. Crime literally does not pay! Clearly the impact upon free will is the same: No one will choose socially evil actions for fear of punishment, and the value of this world is again undermined.

It is important to notice that this argument applies as well to "natural" evil — floods, drought, volcanic eruptions, plague and the like. Imagine a world in which nature responded to man's moral status. The rain falls only on the fields of the righteous; only the wicked are subject to disease; saintly investments average 18% per annum while those of the wicked never yield more than 5%; etc. Again crime does not pay, and righteousness does! And again free will is undermined. To be truly free I must know that I can do evil — I will be neither prevented nor punished — and then exercise my freedom to choose good *because it is good.*

These reflections lead to an important conclusion: *Free will presupposes that God's justice be hidden.* If God intervenes clearly and effectively in human affairs to prevent or repay evil, man loses effective freedom to choose evil. Without freedom to choose evil, there is no *choice* of good either. This means that freedom requires that evil be allowed to occur without interference or punishment, *with all the undeserved suffering which this implies.* Evil claims its victims. What we see now is that there is no alternative: Free will demands that some innocents undergo suffering.

(7) A second good consequence of undeserved suffering is to *clarify the motivation of the righteous.*[6] Their example will inspire the rest of us only if we do not misunderstand them. If their lives go perfectly smoothly, their absolute commitment to the right and the good is hidden behind the obvious self-interested benefit of their righteousness. When we see them suffering and their

---

6. *The Guide of the Perplexed,* III:24; *Duties of the Heart,* IV:3; *Sefer Halkkarim,* IV:13; *Sefer Chasidim,* par. 322.

commitment does not waver, our commitment is strengthened. Furthermore, their steadfastness even in adversity serves to obligate others who might use suffering as an excuse for relaxing moral standards.[7] "I am so poor that I cannot be expected to be honest." "I am in so much pain that I can't be blamed for insensitivity to others." When we see others enduring great pain and privation and whose standards do not fall, these excuses sound hollow. As a result we redouble our efforts.

(8) The Talmud tells us that the suffering and death of the righteous can expiate the guilt of their generation.[8] At first, hearing this sounds strange. We are tempted to ask: "Why should they suffer for the misdeeds of others? They are innocent!" But that question is a mistake. The point of this explanation — and all explanations in the category of future justification — is to show the good which *undeserved* suffering can do. Of course those who suffer are innocent. If they deserved their suffering we would not need to consider future good consequences.

Still, we may feel unsatisfied at the thought of some innocent people suffering in order to protect others. Perhaps a couple of parallels will help. Just before he died, Nathan Hale said: "I regret that I have but one life to give for my country." In other words, he thought it a *privilege* to die, even though he regarded himself as innocent. Why? Because he helped create what he felt was a great good for other people — political freedom. Walter Reed proved that the anopheles mosquito transmits malaria by *intentionally infecting himself.* He didn't *deserve* to suffer and possibly die. But he volunteered in order to help prevent malaria for other people. Generous, idealistic people regard it as a privilege to contribute to a great benefit to others, even if it means pain and danger for We should not think any less of our greatest men and women who are able to shield the rest of their generation from disaster

---

7. Bab. Talmud, *Yoma* 35b.
8. Bab. Talmud, *Moed Katan* 28a; *Shabbos* 33b; *Sanhedrin* 39a. themselves.

(9) Sometimes the future good to which the suffering contributes is for the sufferer himself. Imagine going to the doctor and being told that you have six months to live. Would that change your plans for the next six months? If yes, why? Usually the reason is that with so little time left, you want every minute to be used as well as possible. But isn't that important even if we have many years ahead of us? The value of time is not *really* reduced by having more! But we fall into careless habits of wasting time and opportunities: "I'll get to it next week (year)." Now imagine a miracle cure at the end of six months. Will you regret the scare, the worry and anxiety? Not necessarily. If you think of the impact it had on your ability to focus on the really important aspects of life, you may even be grateful. Some types of suffering have this effect of restoring appropriate focus and thus improving the quality of our lives.[9]

(10) A second personal benefit of suffering is the development of abilities that might otherwise lie dormant.[10] A person with the capacity for heroism may never develop that ability if his life is completely tranquil. A certain amount of adversity is necessary to realize potentialities for courage, compassion, self-sacrifice, stead-fastness, and other similar virtues. This kind of self-development may be regarded as an end in itself: A life of courage, compassion etc. is surely a greater life than one of tranquil mediocrity. And it will contribute to other good consequences as well, e.g., inspiring others, increased reward and so on.

(11) A third personal benefit of suffering emerges if we again consider our judgment that the sufferer is innocent. We are not talking about *perfect* innocence. The sufferer has faults, but *on balance* he doesn't deserve his suffering. Now suppose for a moment we suppress all his positive accomplishments and look

---

9. *Derashos HaRaN* (Jerusalem: 1973), p. 175.

10. *Ramban* to Gen. 22:1, *Ex*. 16:4; see also *Shaar HaGemul*, p. 272 (Heb. ed. Chavel); *Beis Elokim, Shaar HaTeshuvah*, chap. 9; *Sefer HaIkkarim*, IV:13.

only at his failures. Would he then deserve his suffering? Perhaps. If God is taking account only of his misdeeds and disregarding his merits then it may be that his suffering is appropriate for his failures. But why should God do that? The answer given in the Talmud is that he can be freed from liability for those failures in *Olam Haba* (the World to Come).[11] Were we to appreciate the enormous suffering we *avoid* by this exchange, we would regard it as an extraordinary kindness.

(12) Finally, there is the consideration of reward in *Olam Haba* — the World to Come. R. Dessler gives the following analogy.[12] A savage once saved the life of a visiting king. Although they had no common language, the king motioned to the savage to follow him to the palace. They went to the vault where the king stored his precious gems. He gave the savage a sack and indicated that he should fill it with gems. The savage thought: "This is a strange reward. Apparently he wants me to carry these stones for him." He unenthusiastically dropped a few gems in the bag. The king placed the bag on his shoulder and allowed him to leave. The savage rejoiced: "So I don't have to carry a heavy bag of stones. As soon as I am alone I'll ditch it altogether." When he told the story to his friends at home, one of them said: "You fool! Those were jewels which could have made you rich for the rest of your life — and you worried about a few hours' labor lugging a heavy sack?!" Similarly, our suffering can be *infinitely* compensated in *Olam Haba*. From that perspective, our temporary suffering looks like a trivial price to pay for that infinite return.

---

11. Bab. Talmud, *Taanis* 11a; *Kiddushim* 40b; *Yoma* 86b-87a.

12. *Michtav MeEliyahu*, v. 1, pp. 19-23; see also *Emunos V'Deos*, V:3; *Duties of the Heart*, IV:3; R. Bachya on *Ex.* 5:22; *Radak* on *Hosea* 14:10; Bab. Talmud, *Berachos* 5a, Rashi, s.v. *Yisurim Shel Ahavah*.

We have surveyed some of the explanations for suffering. They were of two types. Those related to the past showed that the suffering was really deserved, and hence no problem for our belief in a just God. Those related to the future showed that even if the suffering was undeserved, it created good consequences which justified the suffering. We then claimed that for any realistic case of suffering there is some *combination of principles* by which it could be justified. Evil is only a problem if there are cases of suffering which entirely escape all the principles we discussed. But it is clearly impossible to prove that there is such a case. For it would have to be a case where we know all of the sufferer's private life, the standard of performance against which he should be judged, and whether he has lived previously — in order to judge his relative innocence; and where we know that his suffering is not needed to contribute to God's hiddenness, or to the example of the righteous, to save the generation, to refocus the sufferer's values, develop his abilities, expiate his transgressions or increase his reward in *Olam Haba*. Since we cannot know those things, we cannot prove there is such a case. Thus "the problem of evil" is not insuperable for traditional Judaism.

One final note. We began with three of God's "characteristics" — omniscience, omnipotence and justice. Past justification argues that suffering does not contradict justice. Future justification argues that suffering can be *justified* even if it is *unjust*. We must remember that God is not *only* just; He has other moral attributes as well. For example, God is *merciful*. Now *mercy contradicts a narrow concept of strict justice*. A plea for mercy starts with an admission of guilt: "I know I am guilty and deserve to be punished, but have mercy on me (and don't punish me, or at least mitigate the punishment)." God is also good, and goodness may also contradict strict justice. Strict justice would not allow the righteous to suffer in order to set an example for others, or to contribute to God's hiddenness, but goodness may require it. Past justification sees the problem of evil as *wrong headed* — relying on misinterpretation of the facts; future justification sees the problem as *short sighted* — focusing on strict justice to the exclusion of God's other moral attributes. Together they suffice to solve the problem.

Questions & Answers

LEVEL ONE

In your second principle, you mentioned that our list of responsibilities might not be complete. Could you give me some examples of forgotten responsibilities?

Certainly. We are talking about *Jewish* responsibilities, which means that the entire gamut of Jewish Law is relevant. It is not enough to merely support your family, pay taxes, and refrain from injuring others. There are obligations of charity (approximately 10% of income!), Torah study, Sabbath and Festivals, and endlessly subtle refinements of interactions with others. For example, a creditor must cross the street so as not to meet the one who owes him money, in order not to embarrass him.[13] Business law contains thousands of detailed laws of competition, fraud, fair pricing, etc. Jewish law even regulates emotions and attitudes. I would say that the idea of checking a person against a *complete* list of *Jewish* responsibilities is practically impossible.

You mentioned very briefly that free will enables man to earn his ultimate reward, and that makes the reward itself more valuable. Could you explain this?

---

13. Bab. Talmud, *Bava Metzia* 75b.

Well, this is a very deep subject. I can only give a very inadequate sketch. Let's compare our ultimate reward with charity. Do you know what the highest form of charity is in Jewish thinking? To give the poor person a *job*.[14] Why? Because that does not compromise his dignity and self-esteem. In the same vein, no matter how wonderful that ultimate reward is, if it is not *earned* then it will be imperfect. It will be *undeserved* and hence undermine our self-esteem. Free will solves this problem. But a great deal more needs to be said for this to be really clear.

If free will requires that God be hidden, what about periods when God was open and observable by all, like the generation that left Egypt? They saw the plagues, the crossing of the Red Sea, the pillars of cloud and fire, the manna, not to mention the revelation at Sinai. What happened to their free will?

Excellent question! The answer is: Their free will was much reduced, and this reduced the significance of their lives! The *Meshech Chochmah*[15] explains the Talmudic comment on the verse in Proverbs: "False is charm and empty is beauty" — this refers to the generation of Moses and Aaron. Why? Because their situation *looks* full of charm and beauty due to the open revelation of God they enjoyed. Don't be taken in by that appearance! The enormous reduction in their free will makes the appearance false and empty.

You mentioned Nathan Hale and Walter Reed as parallels to the righteous whose suffering protects their generation. But there is an important difference. Walter

---

15. See Commentary to *Deut.* 32:3.

14. Maimonides, *Hil. Matnos Aniim*, 10:7.

Reed's heroism benefits everyone, and Nathan Hale helped benefit all Americans. The suffering of the righteous benefits a generation which is so guilty that it deserved a catastrophe! Idealism and generosity have limits — must they suffer even to protect the guilty?

You're right, the cases are different. But look at it this way. Suppose your child disobeys your instructions and puts his finger in a fire. As he screams in pain, do you say: "Serves you right!" — or do you try to relieve his pain? Suppose it will cost you time, money, effort and discomfort? The point is that you want to protect those you love, even from suffering which they deserve. The righteous certainly love their fellow Jews enough to want to do this.

I recently read a book on this topic which comes to the conclusion that God can't prevent suffering and therefore He is not all powerful. What do you think of that idea?

Well, it should be clear that I disagree with its conclusions. Let me say first that one must sympathize with the author who was writing out of a deep personal tragedy, honestly trying to make sense out of his experience. But our sympathy must not blind us to the book's shortcomings. I will mention a few problems. (1) The author rejects totally a proposed explanation for suffering if he can find *any* case which it does not cover.[16] But this is unjustified since we use *different combinations* of explanations to cover different cases of suffering. The mere fact that a single explanation does not cover all cases by itself does not make it *irrelevant* to suffering in general. (2) He considers an explanation in valid if, when presented to the sufferer himself, it would

---

16. *When Bad Things Happen to Good People* (Pan: 1981), chap. 1, passim.

not make him feel better![17] Here the author has confused philosophy with pastoral responsibility. Explaining to a heart patient that he suffers from a genetic defect may not make him feel better, *even if it is true*. The same holds for valid explanations of suffering. (3) There is no mention of many of the principles which we have considered. (For example, nos. 2, 3, 5, 7, 8, and 11 are not mentioned at all, and no. 6 is not fully developed, e.g., in relation to natural evil.) This gives the impression that the Jewish sources are unable to face the problem and require a radical revision of Judaism. (His choice is to regard God's power as limited so that He is often *unable* to prevent suffering.) But we have seen that this impression is incorrect. (4) He cites Jacob's prayer (Gen. 32:8) as an example of a request for *strength to bear suffering* — which God can always grant — as consistent with his belief in God's limited power.[18] But Jacob's words are: "Save me, please, from the hand of my brother..." This presumes God *can* save him. (5) The author thinks that mass communication has brought this problem of suffering more to our attention than in previous centuries when tragedies were not instantly reported world wide.[19] When one thinks of infant mortality, diseases like polio, tuberculosis, bubonic plague, starvation and so on, his claim is simply incredible. If anything, our age is *less* sensitive to suffering, or so it seems to me. In sum, the book suffers from faulty logic, poor scholarship and insensitivity. Its popularity is a testimony to the author's writing ability and the lack of good discussions of the topic.

It seems to me that the most difficult suffering to understand is that of children. They are certainly not guilty! How can you explain their suffering?

---

17. Ibid., p. 30-1, 15-6, passim.   18. Ibid., p. 31.   19. Ibid., p. 18-9.

Well, let's look at the principles we discussed. We mentioned in the lecture that reincarnation applies to children — which shows that guilt *is* possible even for them. The necessity for God to hide is also relevant. Imagine a world in which no boy below thirteen and no girl below twelve ever suffered undeservedly. They never fall off their bikes and skin their knees, nor choke on their food, nor burn themselves with matches, etc., etc. Then suddenly at age twelve (for girls) or thirteen (for boys) these things start to happen. This means that we would be constantly surrounded by open miracles, which implies a reduction of free will as I mentioned earlier. Furthermore, the heroism with which even quite young children — from age six, say — face suffering can serve as an example to obligate others. And of course there is always the possibility of compensation in *Olam Haba*. So a number of the principles apply even to what you call the most difficult case.

In the end you appeal to Olam Haba. Isn't this really the whole explanation all by itself? If a person suffers in this world, we must assume that God makes it up to him in Olam Haba — otherwise God is unjust. And once we know He will compensate the sufferer, the objection to the suffering disappears.

This is an excellent question. I think it can be answered if we question the process of suffering in this world in order to increase reward in *Olam Haba*. Remember that we are talking about people who do not deserve this suffering. The question then becomes: Why should they have to suffer in this world in order to increase their reward? Couldn't God give them the extra reward without the suffering? Why shouldn't the righteous enjoy *both* worlds?[20]

---

20. R. Bachya to *Avos*, IV:19.

But then it seems that Olam Haba can never be a justification for suffering. For, we could always protest that he should have been given the extra reward without the suffering!

You're right, if you think of the process as a kind of exchange — suffering for reward — then it makes no sense. But that is not how it is understood. Rather, the suffering is part of the very process by which one becomes worthy of receiving the reward. This is the way the Ramban explains God's testing the righteous.[21] God tests only those He knows will stand the test. Then why bother to test them? Because one deserves more compensation for actions than for mere intention to act. Thus God creates difficult circumstances for them so as to allow them to actualize their good intentions and thus increase their reward. And these circumstances often involve suffering. Now this clearly applies only to a minority of human suffering, and thus cannot be used by itself to solve the whole problem of evil.

You mentioned that reincarnation is obviously relevant to past justification. Well, I'm afraid I can't see the obvious. Suppose in a previous life somebody did something wrong. How can suffering in this life be a punishment if the person doesn't remember what he did and doesn't know that he is now being punished? This especially applies to little children who have no idea at all why they are suffering.

The reason I said the connection is obvious is that the suffering person is no longer *innocent*. That was the problem past justification was supposed to solve, and reincarnation makes it possible that even a newborn is not innocent. But your question can be put another way.

---

21. *Shaar HaGemul*, p. 272.

Granted he is guilty — why is *this* a *meaningful* way to punish him? Surely the punishment should serve some useful purpose. If he can't know why he is being punished, and especially if he is an infant, the punishment looks like sheer vindictiveness. The answer to your question is that even under these conditions, the suffering could be a relevant and useful punishment for the past, because *memory of his past can be restored at a later time*, and at that time he will appreciate the relevance of his suffering to his past misdeeds. It may even be that appropriate punishment *requires* that he be ignorant of the reason for his suffering while it is happening. For example, one type of punishment we often employ with children is to make the wrongdoer experience what he has done to others. ("You took his toy; you lose your toy for today.") In this way he learns what it feels like. Now imagine a pirate who kidnaps infants and sells them as slaves. Those infants experience pain, terror, deprivation, etc., *never knowing why*. How could the pirate experience that? Only if as an infant in a future life he experiences it! Of course *eventually* full memory will be restored and he will *see* the relevance of the punishment to the crime. It may also be that the suffering serves some future purpose. For example, according to many schools of psychology, events or conditions in early childhood can have a lasting effect on the personality. We don't have to agree with the particular details of those theories to accept the general impact of early experiences on development. Now if our pirate's "second childhood" involves painful experiences which leave him timid and shy, those experiences are serving the purpose of correcting his former tyrannical character. Again, in the end he will see why this was necessary. But even now we can appreciate the *relevance* of his suffering.

Questions & Answers

LEVEL TWO

I don't understand the two types of justifications as applied to God. Doesn't Judaism believe that God is good? If so, can the mere fact that someone did something wrong be the reason that he is suffering? That would be mere vengeance! The suffering must always serve some positive purpose, and then everything is justified in terms of future good consequences. In fact, isn't it more correct to understand the whole problem of evil in terms of God's goodness? If He is good (and omniscient and omnipotent), how can He allow suffering?

Your points are very perceptive. Indeed God is good, and that implies that everything must serve a good purpose.[22] And it is true that the problem is often expressed as a conflict between God's goodness and suffering. In fact, at the end of the lecture, I briefly introduced the idea of goodness myself: Future justification is really an appeal to good future consequences. Nevertheless, even though everything must eventually be justified by future good consequences, Judaism still has a limited commitment to past justification in terms of strict justice. The reason is that *the whole system of strict justice contributes to an essential future good, namely our earning our reward.* To

---

22. *The Way of God,* I:2:1.

earn something — to *deserve* something — means that one's *past* actions make that thing appropriate. Therefore this dimension of God's providence serves a higher future purpose reflecting God's goodness. It would require a whole lecture to develop this idea, but I hope this helps. To summarize: Ultimately everything is justified in terms of goodness. Justice and past justification are one aspect of goodness, future justification is another. It is precisely because justice serves the purpose of goodness that future justification can modify what strict justice would otherwise require.

When we shifted to considering the future, you said that many Jewish sources do not stop with the past. Does that mean that some sources do stop with the past?

Very sharp observation! You are quite right, that is exactly what I meant. The *Rambam*, for one, is quite clear that all suffering is deserved.[23] The *Meiri* seems to agree.[24] And the *Ramban* may also agree — the question is how to understand his explanation of testing the righteous. It was with them in mind that I pointed out that logically we could stop with the past. Nevertheless, since so many sources do consider the future (*Emunos V'Deos, Duties of the Heart, R. Bachaya, Rashi, Derashos HaRan, Sefer Chasidim, Radak, Beis Elokim, Sefer HaIkkarim, The Way of God, Michtav MeEliyahu*), it is important for us to understand future justification as well.

I have heard philosophers put the problem of evil in a way which your discussion doesn't seem to touch.[25] The idea is that God knows the future. So, when He considers

---

23. *The Guide of the Perplexed*, III:17, 24.
24. Commentary to *Avos* IV:19.
25. See for example, Mackie, J.L., "Evil and Omnipotence," *Mind* (1955), 209.

creating a particular soul, He knows beforehand what that soul will do. Now why can't God just choose to create those souls which will do good? Of course I mean do good freely — they will face temptation, struggle with themselves, etc. But these souls will win the struggle. Then they will not need corrective suffering — justice for them will require only reward. I understand that this would not relieve all suffering — God's hiding and serving God without ulterior motives require some innocent suffering. But wouldn't the choice to create only souls that will do good result in an enormous reduction in suffering? Wouldn't a God Who is truly good want to create that kind of world rather than ours?

It seems to me that such a world is not possible. You are picturing a world in which no one ever chooses wrongly, and yet man undergoes significant moral struggle so that his free will is meaningful. How does he do this? Can he decide for or against a crime if no one has ever committed the crime? Could he know what the consequences to the victim will be if no one had ever experienced them? And what about individual moral *growth*? Isn't the process of evaluating and rectifying one's mistakes an indispensable part of developing a moral consciousness? How about social responsibility? Can I learn and fulfill an obligation to improve others if no one ever does anything wrong? In sum, I think that a world such as those philosophers describe will result in a drastic reduction in morally significant free will. So your reduction of suffering is not cost free — it requires the sacrifice of much of the supreme value of free will. This is enough to explain why God rejected your type of world.

You said that appeal to the future works because the good created outweighs the evil suffered. It seems to me that another condition is required — that the good could not be achieved any other way. Otherwise we still don't have a reason for God to tolerate the suffering. But now God is all powerful. How can we ever say that God could not have caused that good in some other way, with less suffering?

Your additional condition is quite correct: If the same good is possible without the suffering, then the suffering is not justified. However, God's omnipotence does not automatically mean that we can assume some other means with less suffering was available. First, omnipotence is limited by logic — even God cannot create square circles, married bachelors, or deserved compensation without free-willed effort to earn it.[26] Thus there are limitations even on God's options. That's why I argued against the possibility of a world in which people exercise significant free will and yet no one chooses evil, or God's justice is manifest. It seems to me that these worlds are not possible. Second, remember that the original "burden of proof" is on the objector. He needs to *show* that there was another way possible. To insure that it is really possible, he needs to develop the picture in enough detail so that we can see that no contradiction is hidden in the description. Very often the suggestion of an alternative is plausible only because it is presented in general terms. When we analyze its implications, we realize that in fact it is not possible.

---

26. *The Guide of the Perplexed*, III:15.

Section III

Appreciation
and Application

Prayer,
Petition and Merit

I. *How can prayer (=petition) help? Either I deserve it, in which case I will receive it without asking; or I don't deserve it, in which case I will not receive it even if I ask! Why should God's will to give depend upon prayer?*

II. *How do we maintain self-respect?*

III. *How do we know what to ask for?*

IV. *Prayer parallels sacrifices*

    A. Legal parallels imply common purpose
    B. Prayer is the remainder of the original prayer plus sacrifice institution
    C. Prayer = self-sacrifice in response to judgment in order to induce blessing
    D. Blessing = increase based upon spiritualizing a sample of the category blessed; prayer = self-spiritualization, and preparation to use the requested item correctly (answer to 1)

V. *We ask for means to serve God better (answer to 2).*

VI. *Prayer is a means to achieve what we request — we decide what to request just as we decided what to achieve by other means.*

VII. *Prayer = self-judgment — to evaluate what we truly need for God's service.*

❧ Prayer, Petition and Merit

THE JEWISH PRAYER BOOK GATHERS TO-gether a variety of passages from ancient Jewish texts — the Bible, Mishnah and Talmud are quoted extensively. In addition, there is strictly liturgical material whose origin is in prayer. To analyze the essence of Jewish prayer by searching for the common element in all the passages of the prayer book is an impossible task. Happily, it is also unnecessary: Most of the contents of the "prayer book" is not prayer! Strictly speaking, "prayer" refers to the silent, standing recitation, composed of nineteen blessings on weekdays and seven on Sabbaths and holidays. The various psalms, the Shema and its accompanying blessings, the Scriptural readings, etc., *accompany* prayer, but are not themselves part of prayer.[1] Thus we may restrict our attention to the silent prayer.

The silent prayer is traditionally divided into three portions: praise, petition, and thanksgiving. The reason for this structure is given as follows: When a supplicant approaches his king, it is appropriate for him to praise the king before he presents his case and to thank him afterwards.[2] In other words, the purpose of the audience is petition; praise and thanksgiving are expressions of sensitivity for our relationship to God on the occasion of petition. Thus *the essence of prayer is petition*. This conclusion leads to a number of difficult questions.

(1) *Sefer HaIkkarim* (IV:18) raises a fundamental question concerning the practical power of petition: Either God has decided to give us a particular thing or He has decided not to give it. If He has decided to give it, the request for it is unnecessary; if He has decided not to give it, we will not be able to change His mind by prayer, hence such prayer would be fruitless. In either case prayer is pointless. The point of making any request is to try to get what is requested. If we know beforehand that the request will have no effect on the probability of receiving what is requested, then making the request is a meaningless act. It is clear that this reasoning applies equally to any action designed to change our fortunes at God's hands, and in fact *Sefer HaIkkarim* explicitly includes the performance of all commandments in this challenge of practical impotence. His answer, too, applies generally to the whole field included in the challenge. The answer is that God does not make decrees for *individuals per se*, but rather for groups of individuals meeting certain characteristics. By performing God's commandments we may change our essential characteristics, and thus become a member of a group for whom the Divine decree is preferable. Now this answer applies clearly to commandments in

---

1. See, e.g., Bab. Talmud, *Megillah* 17b.

2. Bab. Talmud, *Berachos* 34a.

general: Obeying God's express command should change one's classification with respect to His decrees. But the application to the case of prayer is less clear. We cannot appeal to the performance of a commandment to pray because (a) before the second Temple (and excluding Maimonides' view) there was no command to pray, and (b) prayer was practiced by the patriarchs before the Torah was given, and they were not specifically commanded to pray. The question thus remains: Why should we expect that asking God for something should affect His decision to give it?

(2) How do we petition God and maintain our self-respect? Is God — even only in part, even only at certain times — the supernatural Supplier of the goodies we, His children, desire? Are our requests for health, wealth, etc., equivalent to a child's request for a candy? Our requests correctly express our total dependence upon God. When we reflect that He made us that way, will this not destroy our dignity?

(3) How do we know *what* to ask for? We all recognize that we may be mistaken about our needs — that we may be seeking what is in fact bad for us; how then do we have the self-confidence to choose what to ask for? Perhaps it would be more realistic to simply accept whatever God gives, trusting His love and His judgment? In order to answer these questions we need to go back to the sources.

The Babylonian Talmud (*Berachos* 26b) states:

> R. Yose ben R. Chanina said that the prayers were established by the patriarchs. R. Yehoshua ben Levi said that the prayers were established (by the men of the Great Assembly) *to correspond with* the sacrifices. There are tannaitic sources supporting both views... One source states: Abraham established the morning prayer... Isaac established the afternoon prayer... Jacob established the evening prayer... Another source states: Why is noon the limit of the morning prayer? Because noon was the limit of

the morning offering... Why is evening the limit of the afternoon prayer. Because evening was the limit of the afternoon offering... Why can the Mussaf prayer be prayed all day? Because the Mussaf offering was offered all day...Let's say this latter source refutes R. Yose ben R. Chanina? R. Yose ben R. Chanina will say that the fathers established the prayers and the rabbis associated them with the sacrifices, for if this is not so, who established Mussaf?

The Talmud here concludes that both traditions are correct: The patriarchs *created the institutions* of the morning, afternoon and evening prayers, but the *obligation* to pray twice daily at certain fixed times with a certain text was initiated by the men of the Great Assembly at the beginning of the second Temple. This means that prayer can exist independently of sacrifices (as it did from the time of the patriarchs), and yet the men of the Great Assembly saw in the previously existing institution some shared essence with sacrifices which guided their new legislation.

This shared essence must be described carefully. Interestingly, the *Shulchan Aruch* (*Orach Chaim* 98:4) cites this Talmudic passage with a slight variation; instead of prayers *corresponding* to sacrifices, they stand *in place of* sacrifices. Taken in isolation such a statement can easily be misunderstood to mean that prayer *replaces* sacrifices *without remainder* — that prayer does all that sacrifices could, and hence that sacrifices are unnecessary. Such an idea is, of course, nonsense. The text of the silent prayer itself pleads for the restoration of sacrifices. Furthermore, the men of the Great Assembly gave legal expression to the relationship between prayer and sacrifices at the *beginning* of the Second Temple. Thus, compulsory prayer existed side by side with sacrifices for more than four hundred years! Obviously, then, prayer was not created as a replacement for sacrifice nor was it ever understood in such a way. But what then does the statement in the *Shulchan Aruch* mean?

There are three different ways in which one thing may be

said to stand in place of another. First, if there is a fly in your soup you can get a new bowl to replace the old. Similarly, the third edition of a book takes the place of the second. This is *replacement without remainder*: The new does (at least) whatever the old did. Second, if there is a train strike, the city may run buses in place of the trains, and if the waiter refuses your order for roast beef because they are all out, he may bring hamburger in its place. This is *replacement by second best*, the new is addressed to the same need as the old, but is not necessarily as effective in meeting it. Third, if the bus carrying the fifteen percent of the choir from out of town fails to arrive, the eighty-five percent will have to sing in place of the whole choir. This is *replacement by remainder*: The new is part of the old and typically less effective in meeting the need in question. The latter is the intention of the *Shulchan Aruch*. The Talmud makes a purely *historical* comment: When the men of the Great Assembly established obligatory prayer they took the legal structure of the sacrifices as their model. The *Shulchan Aruch* is drawing the philosophical implication from the fact: They saw prayer as addressed to the same need as sacrifices, and hence now that we lack sacrifices, *all we have left to address that need is prayer*. There is no implication that sacrifices are unnecessary. On the contrary, since both sacrifices and prayer were directed simultaneously to that need, the loss of sacrifices is a net loss with no replacement. This is the reason that immediately upon the completion of the silent prayer we ask for the rebuilding of the Temple. We are aware that our prayer is only a fragment of a larger, now incomplete, whole; hence we immediately express our longing for its completion.

Now we shall take a closer look at the need to which both sacrifices and prayer were addressed (the "shared essence" mentioned above).

The Babylonian Talmud (*Rosh Hashanah* 16a) states:

[*Mishnah*] At four times the world is judged — on

Passover with respect to grains, on Shavuos with respect to fruits, on Rosh Hashanah all creatures pass before Him like a flock... and on Succos with respect to water.

[*Gemara*] R. Yehuda said in the name of R. Akiva — why did the Torah say to bring the barley offering on Pesach? Because Pesach is the time of grains: God said to bring the barley offering so that the grains of the field may be blessed. And why did the Torah say to bring the *Shtei Halechem* [the Two Loaves offering] on Shavuos? Because Shavuos is the time of fruit: God said to bring the *Shtei Halechem* so that the fruit of the tree may be blessed. And why did the Torah say to pour water (on the altar) on Succos? Because Succos is the time of rain: God said to pour water before Him on Succos so that the rains of the year may be blessed. And (God said:) Say before Me (the prayers of) kingdom, remembrance, and shofar on Rosh Hashanah, in order to accept Me as your King, and that I should remember you for good with the shofar.

If we compare the Mishnah with R. Akiva's exposition, three points are clear. (1) The order in the Mishnah is chronological, while R. Akiva isolated Rosh Hashanah from three major festivals. (2) R. Akiva sees a connection between certain communal sacrifices and the various periods of judgment: Something is to be done with the relevant substance so that there may be a blessing on that substance (as a result of the judgment). (3) Apparently R. Akiva sees the prayer of Rosh Hashanah as parallel to the sacrificial response to the judgments of the major festivals. Prayer on Rosh Hashanah must be the sacrifice of something so that the judgment on Rosh Hashanah will result in a blessing for that something. It is not hard to guess at the "something": *One who prays offers himself as the sacrifice.* But we must probe deeper if we are to understand the connection between sacrifice on the one hand and judgment and blessing on the other, and then apply this to prayer as well.

R. Akiva describes the hoped-for outcome of judgment as *blessing*. The fundamental principle behind the idea of blessing is expressed by *Ramban* (Ex. XXV:24) as follows: ". . .since the world came into existence, God's blessing did not create something from nothing. Instead, the world follows its natural course. . .But when the root of the matter is in existence, blessing comes upon it and increases it, as Elisha said to the woman — II Kings IV:2: (And Elisha said to her: "What shall I do for you? Tell me, what do you have in the house?" And she said: "Your servant has in the house only a cruse of oil." And he said: "Go and borrow vessels from all your neighbors — empty vessels, don't stint. And come and close the door behind you and your children and pour into all those vessels. . ."). . .and the blessing applied to the container of oil and she filled all the vessels. And thus the Table with the Show Bread — blessing will apply to it and from it satiety will come to the whole Jewish people. . ."

Now this is a very difficult passage. It is hard to understand how an open miracle such as Elisha's, even if it is a miracle of *increase only*, could be described as "the world follows its natural order." Nevertheless, the Ramban wants to draw *at least* the following contrast between the period of the creation of the world and the rest of history: During the period of creation things came into existence which formed new species and new categories of existence. Since then we find only repetitions of old species and categories even in the extraordinary process called blessing. *A blessing for a given category must be built on a pre-existing foundation from that category.* But what constitutes a pre-existing foundation? Surely not the mere physical existence of an object of the appropriate type. Notice that the woman had to go home and pour out the oil for Elisha's miracle to work. Nor is physical proximity the key: The Ramban says that the Show Bread is the foundation for a blessing of satiety for all Israel. A foundation for blessing is an object of the appropriate category *with which an appropriate action has been done.* In Elisha's case the appropriate action was pouring the oil *with the faith that the oil would continue to pour.* In the case of the Show Bread the appropriate action is its use in the Temple. Apparently, then, using an object in the Temple is the kind of action which can make that object into a foundation for blessing. This is the connection which R. Akiva expressed when he said: "Why did the Torah say to bring the barley offering on Pesach?. . .so that the grains of the fields may be blessed."

Why does using an object in the Temple transform it into a foundation for blessing? Because that use invests the object with a certain spirituality which then makes possible the spiritual process we call "blessing." The object is used in God's service, thus signifying the recognition that that service is the appropriate end of all resources. As a communal ceremony, it expresses the readiness of the community to use similar resources in similar service (whether in the Temple or elsewhere). It is this resolve for the future, and the dedication of the community to God's service which it implies, which "spiritualize" the sheaf of barley etc. and enable them to initiate the process of blessing.

Prayer does for the individual what the communal sacrifices do for the community. The one who prays engages in Divine service, offering himself to God. He thus signifies his recognition that service of God is the appropriate end of his existence. He expresses his readiness to use all that he has, and all that he is, to that end. *He thus spiritualizes himself and becomes a foundation for the process of blessing which can enter the world through him.* The blessing may apply to his personality — his abilities and talents will increase in power and depth; or it may apply to his possessions or position of power and influence in the world. In any case, it is his dedication of his life to God's service which triggers the spiritual increase called "blessing." Given this understanding of prayer, we can begin to answer our questions. We saw that prayer and the sacrifices have the same essence and the same message: We are prepared to use all that we have and all that we are to do Your will. By making that statement in various ways — some communal, some individual — we render ourselves worthy of the Divine blessing. Since prayer and sacrifices have the same essence and the same function, it was perfectly natural for the men of the Great Assembly to associate them with each other by making them legally parallel. And the association is not merely legal: It is meant to teach us that prayer and sacrifices were integrated into a single coordinated act of dedication to the Divine. Since prayer parallels communal sacrifices in which each individual has a share, prayer gives explicit expression to the individual's participation in the supreme act of national dedication. This is the background for the *Shulchan Aruch's* statement of replacement by remainder: All we have left of this single integrated act is prayer, and so for us prayer alone will have to fulfill the function (however imperfectly) which was once fulfilled by prayer plus sacrifices.

Part of the answer to the question of merit (question no. 1 above) is now clear. If the act of prayer is one of literal self-sacrifice and dedication to God's service, then the one who prays is elevated by that act. He *becomes* more dedicated by expressing his dedication. By acknowledging that all that he is and has must be used for Torah goals, he prepares himself to perceive what God gives him as means to that end. Thus he makes himself more worthy of the Divine blessing: It enables him to "change his category" and thus change his relation to the Divine decree. What is not yet clear is how to overcome the seeming opposition between prayer as self-sacrifice and prayer as petition. How can the verbal formula "(Please) give me health, wealth, etc." be the expression of self-sacrifice? In fact, it seems that petition and self-sacrifice *contradict* one another: In petition I ask God to give to me; in self-sacrifice I offer myself to Him!

The seeming opposition disappears when we reflect on the *content* of our petition. We asked above (question no. 2) whether our requests of God must be seen as the requests of children for the goodies they selfishly desire. They need not be seen in that way *if we request only what we need in order to serve God.* Ultimately, we are asking for His sake, not ours.[3] Perhaps there is shame in asking my employer for higher wages, especially if I know that my job performance does not warrant it. But there is no shame in asking him for better tools with which I can do a better job for him. Thus, for example, the content of the request for income is roughly this: "I offer myself to You — all that I am and all that I have. I am prepared to serve You wholly. Lack of money prevents me from fulfilling many commandments. Help me serve You better by giving me more money." It is obvious that such a request, uttered sincerely, is not in any way shameful. Nor is it inconsistent with self-sacrifice, but rather directly expresses self-sacrifice. Indeed, it is precisely the self-sacrificial context of the request which enables us to maintain our dignity and self-respect.

This explanation of the context of our requests leads directly to our final question (no. 3): If we are asking only for what is necessary to serve God, how do we know what to ask for? Is it not presumptuous of us to pretend to know what we really need? Can we possibly take into account all the consequences of our actions which God deems relevant to determining our future? Of course not. And yet, even though it is presumptuous, and we do not possess all of the relevant information, it is still appropriate for us to rely on our finite and faulty judgment (including consultation with those who guide us) in deciding for what we should pray. The reason is very simple: *Deciding what to pray for is no different in principle from deciding what goals to try to achieve by our own efforts,* and those latter decisions we perforce have to make on our

---

3. Of course, serving God benefits us as well: There is reward in this world and the next, the development and expression of our spirituality which leads to the intense joy of being close to God, and the intrinsic meaning and importance which our lives gain. In the end, however, even though we are conscious of these benefits, we must regard them as wonderful side-products of His service which is done for His sake.

own. Consider income, for example. Should I pray for an increase? Perhaps I am not sure. But now, suppose that I am offered a job paying more money than my present one: Should I take the job? Here I cannot avoid the decision. I must decide to take it or not. If serving God is my ultimate goal, the decision will depend upon whether I think that more money will improve that service. Thus, I *must* make the judgment in the end in order to arrange my practical priorities. If God has put us in a situation where we must make such decisions and act upon them, we are equally justified in applying those decisions to prayer. This is especially clear if we recall the insight of the Chazon Ish that, among other things, *prayer is a form of practical effort.*[4] The Chazon Ish pictures Reuven drowning and Shimon observing him. Since Shimon cannot swim, there is no boat, etc., he decides that there is nothing he can do and walks away. Mistake! There is something he can do *to help* Reuven to shore and save his life: He can pray! We who understand that prayer *is* efficacious must understand it as a practical instrument for changing the world. Thus, the decision to pray for what I think I need to serve God is just another form of deciding *to try to get* what I think I need for that service, and the latter type of decision we certainly have to make.

With this analysis of petition we can understand a profoundly revealing observation of Rabbi S.R. Hirsch. He explains the literal meaning of the Hebrew word for prayer (l'hispalel) as meaning "to judge oneself." At first glance it is hard to find self-judgment in the process of requesting health, wealth, etc., from God. But when we reflect that the request is only for what can improve our service to Him, and that determining what we *truly* need for that service requires profound and searching self-analysis, we see that Rabbi Hirsch's observation reveals an essential aspect of prayer.

---

4. *Sefer Emunah U'Bitachon.*

Questions & Answers

LEVEL ONE

I don't understand why we have a fixed text of prayer. Isn't the point of prayer to express one's true feelings to God? Suppose some of the passages in the prayer book don't move me — isn't it hypocritical to say them without feeling? Why shouldn't each person create his or her own text of prayer? And why does it have to be in Hebrew?

You are right that what is wanted ultimately is completely sincere prayer in which every word *said* is also *meant*. However, there are two ways to achieve this: Adjust the text to fit our feelings, or adjust our feelings to fix the text! Let's remember that the contents of the prayers were set by the men of the Great Assembly, *including the last Jewish prophets*. No one since then could claim comparable religious depth and sophistication. Their text expresses the feelings and thoughts of Jews who possessed real self-understanding and real appreciation of their relationship to God. These are the feelings we *ought* to have: The requests they included ought to be felt by us as our most pressing needs, their words of praise as our overwhelming awe for our Creator, and so on. Now if we don't have those feelings *it is still possible for us to pray sincerely.*

Consider an analogy. The doctor prescribes a medication

and you present the prescription to the druggist. He asks: "Do you really want this? Is your request sincere? Do *you* *feel* the need for this medication?" How should you answer? You feel sick, but you have no direct knowledge of what this medication will do. If you relied on *your* feelings alone, you wouldn't know this medication from a hundred others. Nevertheless, your request is not *insincere*, it is not *hypocritical*. You trust the doctor's judgment and, on his recommendation, you request the medicine *for yourself*. Similarly, we can utter the words of those prophets and sages by relying upon their judgment that these requests express our *real* needs, even if our own feelings would not agree. Simultaneously, we use their text as a test of our progress in developing the appropriate feelings.

One last point — strictly speaking, prayer can be in any language. As long as you don't understand Hebrew, most of your prayer should be in English so that prayer is more than just practicing pronunciation. However, Hebrew concepts cannot be fully translated into any other language, so learning Hebrew should be one of your goals.

Questions & Answers

LEVEL TWO

I have a problem with the text itself. After we list all our specific requests there is a general petition to grant our requests: "Hear our voice, have pity and mercy upon us, receive our prayer with mercy ... do not turn us back empty from before You..." What does this add to the specific requests themselves? And then this is immediately followed by another general petition to accept our prayer with favor: "Be pleased, Hashem our God, with Your people Israel and with their prayer..." What new idea does this contain?

Your questions raise two crucial points. (1) There is, in addition to our specific requests, a petition to be answered, which is not redundant. Consider an analogy. You ask a friend for a loan and he agrees. Two separate things have happened here: You have the money you needed, and *your friend has confirmed your friendship with him by acceding to your request.* Our prayer "...do not turn us back empty from before You..." reflects this second general concern: Answer us so that we may feel Your concern for us and our closeness to You. (2) The following blessing "Be pleased... with their prayer..." expresses the main theme of this lecture. Here the prayer is understood as an offering to God, and we are asking that He accept it with favor.

You said that prayer is a practical means for changing the world. Doesn't that lead to a kind of passivity where people don't take responsibility for their conditions and just pray for God to help them?

If prayer is practically effective, why do you call praying for one's needs a lack of responsibility? But the truth is that you are right: Prayer is meant to accompany other practical measures, not to replace them. We are forbidden to rely upon miracles (Bab. Talmud, *Pesachim* 64b). However we must remember that prayer is not merely the expression of a wish, but a petition designed to help change the world.

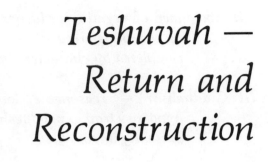

Teshuvah — Return and Reconstruction

I. *Definition — regret, change, confession*

    A. Independence of components

    B. Centrality of confession — religious dimension — repaired relationship with God

II. *Avoidance of negative influence (strategic teshuvah) vs. self-transformation — minimal teshuvah to be completed by character change*

III. *Gradualism — reasonable long-term strategy — hypocrisy trap — valid teshuvah if total change is presently impossible*

IV. *Teshuvah via awe or love; past becomes unintentional or good. Connection?*

V. *Aspects of the Yetzer Hara*

    A. Hates man, wants to kill man, desires specifically what is forbidden, perverse

    B. Very good, necessary for ideal life and joy in learning, *morally blind* yetzer — accidentally evil

    C. Torah dissolves/breaks it, David killed it, God will remove it to a desolate place

    D. Instrument for serving God ("both hearts"), Abraham vs. David, Torah is "spice" for it

VI. *Roughly, repression vs. sublimation explains 4 and 5; (C) used vs. (A) and (B), (D) used only vs. (B); awe → repression, love requires positive use of all capacities*

VII. *Steps to teshuvah — partial, strategic, from awe, from love.*

۶§ *Teshuvah* — *Return and*
Reconstruction

TESHUVAH IS THE JEWISH PROGRAM FOR
dealing with personal failure. (*Teshuvah* is often translated as *repentance*; we will see immediately that this is
inadequate. Since there is no English word which
captures the full connotation of *teshuvah*, it is better to use the
original Hebrew.) In the classical sources, teshuvah has three
necessary components: (1) regret for past misdeeds, (2) resolution
not to repeat them in the future, and (3) confession (to God).[1] Let us
examine these components and their relationships to one another.

---

1. Maimondes, *Hil. Teshuvah*, 2:2; R. Yona, *Shaarei Teshuvah*, 1, Halkar
HaChamishi; *Sefer HaChinuch, mitzvah* 364.

Regret for past actions involves (at least) the judgment that those actions were wrong and a feeling of pain (guilt, embarrassment, disappointment, etc.) as a result of having done them. Notice that regret does not imply the second component — resolution to change future actions. A person may say: "I know what I did was wrong, and it hurts me to think that I do that sort of thing, but my desire to do it is so strong that I cannot guarantee my future actions." His regret is sincere, but he has not resolved to change. It is equally true that the second component does not imply the first. A person may decide to change his actions because of a change in conditions — they have become too dangerous or costly — without regretting the past at all. So the first two components of teshuvah are completely independent of one another. The third component is also independent of the first two — one can regret the past and resolve to change the future without verbalizing these experiences at all.

Are the components equally important? Or are some more fundamental than others? Many, I think, would answer that (1) and (2) are much more fundamental than (3). Regret and resolution are the basic changes in the personality in which we come to grips with the problem. Confession, it seems, is just a verbalization of these inner events. It might serve to strengthen one's resolve, or make one's regret more vivid, but it is hard to see its fundamental importance. It is therefore interesting that the sources agree that verbal confession is necessary for teshuvah, and some go so far as to make a verse in the Torah describing *confession* the source for the entire mitzvah![2]

In order to understand the centrality of confession, notice that *regret and resolution have no necessary connection to religion* — they may occur to an atheist! A smoker about to have a lung removed may say: "What a fool I was! My smoking cost me a lung

2. Maimonides, *Sefer HaMitzvos*, pos. *mitzvah 73*; *Hil. Teshuvah, 1:1*; *Sefer HaChinuch* #364.

— it was wrong, I shouldn't have done it. And of course I will stop smoking; I can't afford to endanger my other lung!" Religion need not come into this experience at all. The importance of confession is that it reveals the essence of teshuvah as a religious event. That essence is *return to God*. Our misdeeds are seen as damaging ourrelationship to God; teshuvah is the repair of that relationship. Confession is fundamentally important because it alone demonstrates the religious character of teshuvah. (Now we see why translating *teshuvah* as *repentance* is incorrect: The religious essence of teshuvah is lost.)

In order to understand the components of teshuvah more precisely, let's look at Maimonides' *Laws of Teshuvah*, chapter 2, paragraphs 1 and 2. In paragraph 1 he says: "What is complete teshuvah? It is confronting the same situation in which he failed, being able to do the same again, and yet acting rightly due to teshuvah — not from fear or lack of strength." In paragraph 2 he says: "And what is teshuvah? The sinner must abandon his sin, remove it from his thought and resolve in his heart not to do it again... Also, he must regret the past... And he must confess verbally what he has resolved in his heart." These statements of Maimonides raise two questions. (a) What is the difference between teshuvah (paragraph 2) and complete teshuvah (paragraph 1)? Is it just the fact that he underwent the test? If there is no *inner* difference, why is the teshuvah more complete? b) Why does Maimonides explain *complete* teshuvah before teshuvah? In discussing a new concept doesn't it make sense to define the concept *before* introducing "complete" forms of the concept?

The first question can be answered if we consider the following case. Fred lived in Auckland, New Zealand. With him in Auckland lived someone — Mr. X — with whom Fred could not get along. Mr. X irritated Fred and brought out the worst in him. Although he berated himself for his inappropriate behavior, Fred simply did not control himself. Finally he found a solution to his problem. Fred moved to Reykjavik, Iceland! Out of Mr. X's way,

Fred's behavior immediately improved. This was satisfactory until Fred saw in the society pages of *The Reykjavik Times* that Mr. X was also moving to Reykjavik. Fred promptly moved to Los Angeles. The situation is at present stable, though Fred carefully follows the society pages of the *Los Angeles Times*. Fred has solved his problem by avoiding the temptation which he did not overcome. But has he done teshuvah? I see from your expressions and shaking heads that many of you feel that Fred has not done teshuvah. I sympathize with your feeling. His "solution" seems not to confront the real problem which is his failure to *control his behavior* in Mr. X's company. A real solution, it seems, would enable Fred to develop the requisite self-control. But let's test Fred's solution against the necessary components of teshuvah. (1) Has Fred sincerely regretted his past behavior? It certainly seems so; there is no reason to think his self-criticism is insincere. (2) Has Fred resolved to change his future behavior? Again it certainly seems so — the effort and expense of running around the globe in order to keep away from Mr. X indicates a sincere (and so far successful) resolve not to repeat his past mistakes. Finally, (3) we may assume that Fred has confessed his actions to God. So Fred has all the necessary components — *Fred has done teshuvah!*

Indeed, Fred has done *teshuvah*, but not *complete* teshuvah. He has not "confronted the same situation in which he failed and acted rightly." We now see a crucial difference between the two: The requirements of *teshuvah* can be satisfied by systematically *avoiding* temptation, whereas *complete* teshuvah requires achieving the self-control to *overcome* the temptation. Teshuvah is primarily a matter of changing *behavior*; *complete* teshuvah requires changing *motivation*, and ultimately, changing one's *character*. Question (a) is answered; complete teshuvah is not just a practical test of teshuvah, but rather requires a change of character guaranteeing that the resolve of teshuvah can stand the test.

Let's turn now to question (b): Why does Maimonides start with complete teshuvah? Notice that the relationship between teshuvah and complete teshuvah can be understood in two different ways. Complete teshuvah might be teshuvah plus the requirement of character change, or teshuvah might be complete teshuvah minus that requirement. In other words, the additional requirement might be considered an "extra credit" addition to an already self-sufficient teshuvah; or we may consider only complete teshuvah as self-sufficient, with teshuvah as an incomplete form (which is nevertheless enough for certain purposes). The difference will show in our attitude towards teshuvah. Is it enough to do teshuvah, with complete teshuvah as an independent extra option? Or is teshuvah itself incomplete, needing supplementation in order to fulfill its true purpose? I think the latter is correct: Control of behavior, in addition to its own intrinsic value, is meant to lead ultimately to change in character. To stop at the first stage is to fail to realize its true potential as the foundation for complete teshuvah. This is the reason that Maimonides starts with complete teshuvah: This is the *goal* of teshuvah; teshuvah itself is incomplete — this is what follows from defining it in paragraph 2 after the explanation of complete teshuvah.

This means that complete teshuvah may be reached by a two-step process: (a) control of behavior with teshuvah, and then (b) reformation of the personality. Indeed, in some cases this may be the only way to achieve complete teshuvah. As long as the wrong behavior is performed habitually it is continuously reinforced. The motivation for the behavior remains strong and therefore very difficult to control. Ceasing the behavior, even by avoiding temptation, allows the motivation to "cool" and become more manageable.

Reaching complete teshuvah in two steps illustrates a general approach to teshuvah: *gradualism*. Teshuvah is seen as a *process*, rather than an all-or-nothing achievement. Even incomplete teshuvah can be achieved in stages of gradual change of behavior.

In order to understand this process, let's analyze the steps along the way.

What is the status of *partial* teshuvah? Someone has a problem with a certain area of behavior. He could control it under some circumstances but not, he feels, under others. Such a person may think that a partial change of behavior is *hypocritical*. If he really believed that the behavior is wrong, he would not permit it to himself *at all*. Therefore, to be really honest and sincere, he should not change at all until he can change *consistently and completely*. For example, many have said: "I would like to keep kosher, and it would be easy for me to do — at home. But business luncheons and social gatherings are something else. I can't embarrass myself by refusing to eat or bringing my own food. So, for the time being, the best I can do is to keep 80% kosher. But that is hypocritical — if you believe in kashrus you should keep it all the way. Whatever other failings I have, I am not a hypocrite! Therefore I will wait until I have the will power to keep kosher 100%."

I call this argument the Hypocrisy Trap. It is a trap because it has no validity. To see this, let's consider a parallel case. Fred has a severe allergy to chocolate; his doctor has told him to cut it out completely. But every lunch hour Fred's boss makes the rounds with a box of chocolates and won't take "No" for an answer. Fred is not prepared to jeopardize his job, so one chocolate a day he cannot avoid. Shall he therefore eat chocolate at home in order to avoid the "hypocrisy" of not swearing off chocolate 100%? Surely not: He should do the best he can. Each bite of chocolate is a separate liability for his allergy. His inability to control his boss at lunch is no reason to add to his problem at home. Similarly with respect to kashrus — each meal, each bite of food, is a separate action with its own significance. The inability to control one's social diet is no reason not to control the rest.

But what of the charge of hypocrisy? Isn't a hypocrite someone who says he believes in something and then fails to live it in practice? *No* — a hypocrite is someone who says he believes in something and then *does not make an honest effort* to live it in practice. Phillip is a heavy smoker who condemns smoking unequivocally. Nevertheless, he still smokes. When questioned concerning the contradiction between his words and his actions, he replies: "I attend anti-smoking group-therapy sessions every week, I have had hypnotic treatments and tried drugs. I'm trying!" Phillip is obviously *not* a hypocrite.

Thus partial teshuvah is *always appropriate* — the improved behavior is a net gain for one's life as a whole. But is partial teshuvah valid *as teshuvah*? Does it meet the three conditions? Regret and confession may be assumed; the problem is with resolve to change the rest of the behavior. That depends upon whether one has the *ability* to change the rest. If one is incapable of controlling the rest of his behavior then his resolve to change what he can is valid, and thus his teshuvah is valid. And even if he could change the rest of his behavior, but is just rationalizing, he still has the benefit of the partial behavioral improvement. Furthermore, that partial improvement can be the key to finishing the job. Even small improvements add to self-control, increase self-confidence, and create a momentum which naturally leads to further progress. Thus partial teshuvah is an important first step in the teshuvah process.

Teshuvah naturally effects one's future — at the very least one's actions will be different. But teshuvah also has an effect on the past. As we shall see in detail shortly, teshuvah frees us from liability for our past actions. Under certain conditions, actions which were intentional transgressions become as if they were unintentional, or even as if they were meritorious! This appears paradoxical: How can anything I do now change the character of the past? I don't know the answer to this question. Perhaps it is simply an extraordinary kindness that God promises those who do teshuvah. Nevertheless, we can investigate the *specific conditions* under which *specific changes of the past* take place. The Talmud makes the following statement[3]: "If one does teshuvah out of awe of God, his intentional transgressions become as if they were unintentional; if he does teshuvah out of love of God, they become as if they were *mitzvos* — good deeds." How shall we understand the link between the two types of motivations for teshuvah and the two different effects on the past actions?

First we need to describe the two types of teshuvah. Awe is a sense of overwhelming greatness, goodness, meaning and significance. Awe implies respect and reverence, with a sense of smallness and distance. Imagine yourself in the presence of a person for whom you feel awe, reverence, etc. Many of the temptations to which you regularly succumb would lose their power over you — in front of such a person you would muster the will power to resist. Now our goal is to feel the presence of God continuously.[4] This implies the greatest awe conceivable, and thus can be the motivation for teshuvah.

That love can motivate teshuvah is also clear. Everyone recognizes that love is very precious. If two people are in love and one realizes that certain actions will jeopardize that love, he has a powerful reason to change those actions. This is all the more true of love of God. So we understand that awe and love can motivate teshuvah. But still the link with the specific changes of the past mentioned in the Talmud is not explained. In order to understand that link, we need to examine the psychological difference between the two types of teshuvah.

The description of human motivation in classical Jewish sources begins with the conflict between the Good and Evil Intentions. When we analyze those sources in particular with respect to the Evil Inclination, we find a profound ambiguity. There seem to be two conflicting *descriptions* of the Evil Inclination, and two conflicting *policies* for dealing with it.

---

3. Bab. Talmud, *Yoma*, 86b.
4. *Shulchan Aruch, Orach Chaim*, 1:1.

Description #1: The Evil Inclination hates man, wants to kill man, and desires specifically what is forbidden *because* it is forbidden.[5]

Description #2: "And God saw all that He had made and behold it was very good..." — "good" is the Good Inclination; "very good" is the Evil Inclination![6]

Policy #1: The Torah dissolves or breaks the Evil Inclination; God will eventually remove it to a desolate place; King David killed his Evil Inclination.[7]

Policy #2: "You should love God with all your heart" — with *both* your "hearts", i.e., your Good *and* Evil Inclinations; God found both Abraham's hearts faithful before Him. (King David killed his Evil Inclination only because he could not reach Abraham's achievement of making it faithful to God.)[8]

According to Description 1 the Evil Inclination rebels for the sake of the rebellion itself. "Stolen waters are sweet"[9] — their being stolen is what makes them sweet. If the owner gives permission to drink them they lose their sweetness! Such a desire seems the very epitome of evil. Yet Description 2 declares that the Evil Inclination is the "very" of "very good". How can this be? According to Policy #1, we look forward to utter dissociation from the Evil Inclination, either by destroying it or distancing it from ourselves. Policy #2 envisions using the Evil Inclination in our service of God. Isn't this a contradiction?

These questions are answered in classical sources[10] by

---

5. Bab. Talmud, *Kiddushim* 30b; *Succah* 52a-b; *Nedarim* 91; *Sanhedrin* 75; Jer.Talmud, *Nedarim* 9:2.

6. *Gen. Rabbah* 9:7; *Zohar* 138a.

7. Bab. Talmud, *Niddah* 30b; *Succah* 52a; Jer. Talmud, *Sotah* 5:5.

8. *Deut.* 6:5, *Rashi*; Jer. Talmud, *Sotah* 5:5, *Michtav MeEliyahu*, v.3, p. 148ff.

9. *Proverbs,* 9:17.

10. *Michtav MeEliyahu*, v.1, p. 71, v.2, p. 33, v.4, p. 133; H., Goldberg, *Israel Salanter* (New York: 1982), p. 163f.

distinguishing two different aspects of the Evil Inclination and applying the policies to them selectively. Description 1 refers to the perverse "evil for Evil's sake" aspect of the Evil Inclination. However there is another aspect which is evil because it is *morally blind*. It has no knowledge of moral distinctions and hence will often desire evil due to its ignorance. Take for example the desire to enjoy food. It makes no difference to that desire whether today is a fast day (in which case the enjoyment is forbidden), or a holiday (in which case the enjoyment is a mitzvah), or an ordinary day (in which case the enjoyment is optional). This aspect of the Evil Inclination is capable of leading to good actions as well as evil actions. It is called "evil" because, left to itself, it will surely lead sooner or later to evil through its moral blindness.

The two policies apply to the two aspects of the Evil Inclination as follows. Only Policy #1 is relevant to the perverse aspect. Since this aspect desires evil because it is evil, we can only dissociate ourselves from it. We cannot use it in serving God because as soon as we find a context in which what it desires is no longer evil, it ceases desiring it. On the other hand, with respect to the morally blind aspect, *both policies are relevant*. It is possible to dissociate from it. But it is also possible to guide it in such a way that it contributes to one's service of God since its desire for evil is merely "accidental" and not perverse.

Since both policies can be applied to the morally blind aspect of the Evil Inclination, we must ask which policy is preferable. The answer is: Policy #2. As we saw above, King David killed his Evil Inclination only because he was not able to elevate it to God's service as Abraham did. (This could only refer to the morally blind aspect since the perverse aspect is inherently incapable of serving God.) Furthermore, there are cases in which only Policy #2 is possible as a long-term resolution of the morally blind aspect of the Evil Inclination. The reason is that man is not "infinitely plastic". Certain aspects of a person's character cannot be changed or permanently denied. The Talmud[11] describes a certain group of people who must shed blood. Some will become murderers, others *shochtim* (slaughterers providing kosher meat), and still others *mohelim* (those who perform circumcision). Although they all shed blood, one is society's worst enemy, another performs a needed service, and the third performs one of the most important mitzvos. However, if such a person becomes a librarian, one day someone will return an overdue book — out will come the scissors and...! Now for those aspects of character which cannot be changed or permanently denied, Policy #1 is obviously im-possible as a long-term solution; thus Policy #2 is our only option.

The superiority of Policy #2 should not lead us to discard Policy #1 entirely. There are times when Policy #2 is simply too difficult to implement — even a King David can fail. Furthermore, Policy #1 may be a *necessary first step* before Policy #2 can be used. As long as the negative motivation is freely expressed in behavior, it may be impossible to constructively channel the motivation. It may be necessary first to suppress the motivation *temporarily* to gain control of behavior. Then it can be channeled gradually into conditions where it is positive. Compare trying to attach a hose to a spigot which is turned on full force. It can't be done. First it must be shut off. Then when the hose is attached the water can be directed at will.

Now we are in a position to try to explain the Talmudic connection between the motivations for teshuvah and the changes of the past. Let's analyze the two types of teshuvah psychologically. When motivated by *awe* the person is divided against himself. Part of him wants to perform the wrong action, another stronger part is aware of God's presence and filled with an awe which restrains him. The urge to evil is denied expression. *If we measure his past actions against his present psychology we must*

---

11. Bab. Talmud, *Shabbos* 156a; see Gra on *Proverbs*, 22:6.

regard these actions as unintentional; as he is now, he would not do such things.

This much is also true for a person who does teshuvah out of love. The part of him which prizes the love will be set against the urge to evil and may overcome it. But there will be an additional factor. Love cannot be content with merely overpowering the negative motivation. For, *the very existence of the negative motivation damages love.* Love is a relationship which seeks to involve the whole person. As long as that negative motivation exists, even if it is never expressed in action, a part of his personality will be excluded from the love relationship, and thus the love will be partly frustrated. To do teshuvah out of love of God requires finding a a way to incorporate the "negative" motivation into that love. The result is a wholly integrated personality, as opposed to the inner division produced by awe. This is an application of Policy #2. *If we now measure his past actions against his present psychology we will see that those actions make a contribution to his present and future service of God.* Thus they can be regarded as being valuable instead of wholly evil.

Perhaps an analogy will help clarify these different relationships to the past. Imagine someone growing up in the slums of Chicago, joining a youth gang and becoming its leader. For several years, the gang carries out vicious exploits under his direction. When he matures, he regrets his past. Now he may become an accountant and lead a peaceful, law-abiding life. He is no longer a person who would engage in those activities — his present psychology is disconnected from those past actions. But suppose instead that he becomes a policeman and specializes in juvenile work. Then his past exploits contribute directly to the good he does now (and in the future). Those actions which were evil at the time now become the foundation for continuing good; his present psychology is not disconnected from the past, but rather benefits directly from it. These constructive consequences of the past actions are registered by the Talmudic statement that they become "as if they were *mitzvos*."

Teshuvah motivated by love is the highest form of teshuvah, and can be seen as the culmination of a gradual, step-by-step process:

(1) Partial teshuvah — changing that part of one's behavior which one can directly control.

(2) Teshuvah — changing all of one's behavior, even if only by systematically avoiding conditions of temptation.

(3) Complete teshuvah — changing one's motivation so as to be immune to temptation.

(4) Teshuvah out of love — elevating one's "negative" motivation so that it contributes to one's service of God. Each step leads to the next. Changing part of one's behavior increases self-control and motivation so that one can finish the process and change the rest. Getting control of behavior decreases reinforcement of negative motivation so that stronger positive motivation can take control and complete the teshuvah. Once the negative motivation is completely under control a constructive use for it can be sought, as is required for teshuvah motivated by love.

Questions & Answers

LEVEL ONE

You said that a person could sincerely regret his past actions without resolving to change. I don't see how that is possible. If his regret is really sincere, how can he plan to continue to act in the same way again?

If the regret is sincere, that surely gives him *a* reason to change. The trouble is that it is only *one* reason — one motivation — among the many which move him to act. He may feel that he has other motivations which counterbalance his regret, leaving the action in the realm of his will, and he cannot guarantee that his will will choose correctly. There is no reason to assume that sincere regret will automatically be our strongest motivation.

You explained the impact of the different types of teshuvah by measuring the past actions against present psychology. But why should we measure in this way? After all, the past action is part of history — if I murdered someone, my teshuvah can't bring him back to life!

You are quite right — teshuvah cannot literally change the past. That's why I said that I cannot explain how the moral character of those actions should be affected by what I do now. Perhaps this is what Isaiah is referring to (55:8) when he exhorts the evil person to do teshuvah, and then says: "For My thoughts are not your thoughts, nor are your ways My ways..." According to *your* thoughts and ways the past is closed, but *My* thoughts and ways are different. The idea of measuring past actions against present psychology is only a way of describing the relevant difference between the types of teshuvah. I can't prove that we must measure this way, but this measurement may explain how the Torah makes the distinction.

You described love as not tolerating the exclusion of any part of the personality. From this you concluded that only Policy #2 was relevant to implementing teshuvah out of love — some way of incorporating the "negative" motivation into the love relationship. But it seems to me that Policy #1 could accomplish the same thing: If you eliminate the negative motivation then it will not be there to be excluded from the love. The personality can then be completely integrated into the love relationship.

That is an excellent observation. You are right — if we look at the end result, Policy #1 could provide an undivided personality. However, we must remember that *in the process* something is lost. We are imagining a part of the personality obliterated, something like a lobotomy. Will love easily tolerate that loss? That way there is less of the person to love and be loved. I think that love demands *rehabilitation* of the motivation rather than its elimination.

Questions & Answers

LEVEL TWO

You asked why Maimonides discusses complete teshuvah before teshuvah. Isn't the problem worse than that? He actually uses teshuvah to describe complete teshuvah in Paragraph 1 — before we even know what teshuvah is (from Paragraph 2)! He says: "What is complete teshuvah? It is confronting the same situation in which he failed. . . and acting rightly due to teshuvah. . ."

That is correct, and it increases the need for the explanation that the teshuvah of pragraph 2 is only a stop on the road to complete teshuvah.

You said that teshuvah has only three necessary conditions: regret, resolution to change and confession. But I have heard that there are more conditions. For example, if someone stole something, he is required to return the stolen object or make restitution.

And there is another condition, that we must approach the person we have wronged and ask his forgiveness.

Your statements are not quite correct: Returning stolen property and placating those whom we have wronged are both necessary for *forgiveness and absolution,* i.e., *kaparah,* but not for teshuvah.[12] For transgres-

---

12. Maimonides, *Hil. Teshuvah,* 2:9.

sions between man and God (where no other person is affected), one need only do teshuvah in order to gain kaparah[13]; if another person is affected, then the conditions you mentioned are also required. And I think we can see the relevance of those additional conditions since they are natural extensions of regret and resolution to change. Think of it this way. A person who regrets his actions and resolves to change is saying: "I wish I had not acted that way, and if I had it to do over I would act differently. However, since I cannot go back in time, at least I will not repeat the mistake in the future." Now suppose that some of the consequences of the past action exist and will continue into the future unless he corrects them. It is a natural extension of his statement to apply his resolve to those consequences and require him to eradicate them. Both returning the stolen object (or repairing any other damages) and soothing bruised feelings are necessary to undo what is left of the transgression.

---

13. Although teshuvah is all the guilty party must *do*, there are other things that must happen for *kaparah* to be granted for certain kinds of transgressions. See Maimonides, *Hil. Teshuvah*, 1:4.

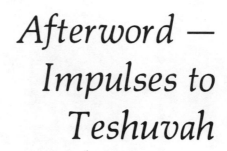

*Afterword —
Impulses to
Teshuvah*

◄§ Impulses to Teshuvah

T HE LECTURES AND DISCUSSIONS THAT HAVE been recorded in this book represent a sample of twenty years' teaching experience. During that time I have tried to communicate the fundamentals of contemporary Jewish philosophy in a very wide variety of contexts — regular lectures at Yeshivat Ohr Somayach and Neve Yerushalayim Seminary in Jerusalem, lectures and Shabbatons in the United States, Canada, the United Kingdom, and South Africa. The audiences contained a wide variety of people. Ages ranged from eighteen to eight-five. Secular education varied from high school through medical doctors, Ph.D.s and various professions. There were the cultural differences between five countries on four continents. And their attitudes towards Judaism included curiosity, skepticism, personal exploration, disbelief, developing commitment, and bitter hostility. One factor, however, they all shared: a sincere desire to increase their knowledge and understanding of traditional Judaism. This desire has made for an educational experience of unparalleled intensity. People who seek education not merely to please their parents, or to increase their income, but because they need to make informed life-decisions, give classes a unique focus and meaning. Many of these people have continued their exploration of Judaism with a period of full-time study, and some with a commitment to traditional Judaism as a way of life. In this "Afterword" I will try to give the reader an insight into the lives of a few of those who have taken this seemingly radical step. Perhaps the reader will find more points of comparison with them than might be assumed.

What moves people to investigate traditional Judaism as a possible life commitment? I am not a sociologist, and I have not done a formal survey, but twenty-five years of personal experience has led me to recognize two very common motivations. One is the desire to investigate roots. I was born a Jew — what does that mean? What is a Jewish identity? This desire is often coupled with a painful realization of ignorance, and a suspicion that previous sources of information have not been wholly accurate. The second is a quest for a certain kind of personal growth — to incorporate ideals, meaning and integration into one's life. The goal is to contribute to a universal value based upon objective truth, rather than merely chase personal pleasures. These motivations vary in strength and style from person to person. Nevertheless, some shared elements can be described, together with the kinds of responses which will help satisfy the inquirer's need.

1. *Roots*. Consider Joseph*, a graduate of Yale Law, from a Conservative Jewish background in the United States. What drew

---

* Names and inessential details have been changed in order to insure anonymity.

him to yeshivah study in Jerusalem was the puzzle of martyrdom. He was aware that throughout the millennia, millions of Jews have died rather than give up Judaism. According to his Jewish education, Judaism consists of outmoded superstitions and anti-quated, irrelevant customs. Why would anyone die for *that?* (Of course, he could simply have dismissed them all as misguided. Instead he realized that he must be missing Judaism's essential meaning.)

Or consider Uri.* Raised on a non-religious kibbutz, Uri had no knowledge of, or interest, in Jewish tradition. He qualified as a lifeguard and took a job at another non-religious kibbutz. When he arrived to take up residence, he was given a tour of the premises. He saw the dining hall, the pool, the cow shed, the chicken coop, etc. Finally he was introduced to a pig which the kibbutz had named Abraham. "A pig — Abraham?!" he exclaimed. That shocked him. But then he reflected: "Why am I shocked? What do I believe in? What is Abraham to me?" Nevertheless, he could not make peace with such contempt for the first Jew.

Both Joseph and Uri eventually arrived at Ohr Somayach to explore their roots in depth. What kinds of response are useful for someone engaged in such an exploration? Although there may be many others, I find three to be especially important.

A. Jewish history. The unique experience of the Jewish people over 3500 years needs to be portrayed with its essential themes identified. Historians have not the vaguest ideas how to explain Jewish survival, especially during the last 2000 years of exile. And it is not "Jewish identity" or "Jewish cultural products" which survive: Jews have been involved in assimilationist movements throughout our history and those movements have *not* survived. No — what survives is a specific way of life. Certain values, beliefs, behaviors, literary sources and character types seem historically indestructible. The uniqueness of the Jewish world-view in the ancient world — one God embodying absolute power, ideally ethical and demanding human moral striving; human brotherhood leading to world peace and cooperation — is also without explanation. Examining these and other historical topics is a crucial step to a Jewish identity.

B. Contributions to world civilization. By any measure the Jewish contribution to human life and thought is awesome. But with monotheism and morality, Judaism gives the foundation of a world-view and the essential agenda for the future. When it is appreciated that both these elements are of Jewish origin, world history takes on a different aspect: The world steadily becomes more and more Jewish!

C. Quality of life in traditional Jewish communitites. Statistics show that these communities are favorably distinguished from their surroundings in many important respects, including violent crime, drug addiction, divorce and family relations, literacy and general intellectual development. (Note that perfection is *not* claimed, only favorable distinction.) These differences represent traditional Judaism in practice. The record indicates possession of practical wisdom which again has no historical explanation.

These three responses go a long way towards instilling pride in one's Jewish identity, and a desire to develop that identity further.

2. *Personal growth.* Here are two conversations from my personal experience. The first took place at a Jewish fair in Baltimore. The person to whom I was speaking — call him Fred — exuded a magnificent contentment, self-confidence, self-satisfaction. I wondered that a person could be so happy with his status quo.

> D.G.: "Have you no goals for personal growth, no ideals of self-improvement to which you aspire?"
> Fred: "Nope."
> D.G.: "But surely you are not perfect!"

Fred: "Oh, of course not!"

D.G.: "But look — if you had a problem with your business, you would study it, hire experts, etc., and work to solve it. The same with your health. Why don't you want to improve yourself as a person?"

Fred: "You're right, Rabbi — in business or health I would try to improve the situation. But when it comes to myself as a person, I accept myself as I am. I am happy, I sleep well, I am content not to be better than I am."

At this point I was searching desperately for some way to reach Fred and show him the shallowness of his outlook.

D.G.: "Fred, do you have children?"

Fred: "Yes, two sons aged fourteen and ten."

D.G.: "Imagine that your fourteen-year-old is caught shoplifting by the police. When you confront him, he admits it. Moreover, he tells you that he intends to continue (more carefully, of course). 'But don't worry Dad,' he adds, 'I am happy, I sleep well, I am content not to be better than I am.' What would you answer him?"

Suddenly Fred remembered a pressing appointment and broke off the conversation.

The second case concerned a professor of engineering at a West Coast university — let's call him Bob.

Bob : "Congratulate me — I just got a government grant!"

D.G.: "Congratulations! That's wonderful! Tell me, from which agency did you get it?"

Bob : "It is an anti-pollution project."

D.G.: "Anti-pollution? I didn't know you were working on anything like that."

Bob : "I'm not."

D.G.: "But then how did you get the grant?"

Bob : "Well, they need to build a certain machine. I told

them that in order to build the machine, they need to rarefy a certain gas. To rarefy the gas they need a special electric current, and I am building a component to produce the current. They bought the story, so now I can complete my research!"

For once, I couldn't think of anything to say.

These conversations express an attitude of cynicism, anti-idealism and lack of personal aspiration, which is very widespread. Certain people find such an attitude appalling. "The unexamined life is not worth living," said Socrates. And the purpose of examination is not mere passive understanding; it is improvement. A person's life is measured not only by what he has *done*, but also by what he has *become*. I myself — my personality, my character, my very identity — am one of my chief responsibilities, one of my most central projects. And my actions must express and contribute to my life's meaning and value.

For people with such goals and values, it is a delightful discovery that traditional Judaism shares their concerns in full. They find a philosophy and a variety of programs of self-evaluation and growth. Even more important, they find people who have incorporated these values into their lives. A crucial response to this motivation is to introduce the inquirer to such people — personally, if possible, or through biographies. Stories such as those I cited in "The Chosen People" illustrate the aspirations of the traditional Jew. It is also beneficial to describe the consciousness achieved by people like themselves who have decided to adopt a traditional life-style. As one fellow told me:

I had a shock this morning. A few days ago my wife gave birth to our third son. I was preparing something to say at the bris. I am not a public speaker. The very thought of standing in front of an audience makes me panic. Well, as I was planning my speech it hit me. Whatever I say, however I speak, it will be done in a few minutes and in a few days forgotten. And for *that* I am petrified. But every morning when I get up to *daven* (pray) before the King of kings — that doesn't make me nervous at all! Something is very wrong here...

I met a woman in the second year of law school. Her commitment to Judaism was only a few years old. When I asked her what area of law she would specialize in, she told me:

The truth is, I really like trial law. I debate well, the psychology of the courtroom fascinates me, and I am by nature a competitive person. But lately I have begun to have doubts. Since I have become committed to traditional Judaism I have been thinking about my *midos* (character traits). The competitiveness and agressiveness of the courtroom will not contribute to the person I want to become. Until I make my decision I'm exploring tax law as well.

Another fellow, already ten years into his commitment explained to me how his understanding of self-examination developed:

At first, when I heard about Yom Kippur, I was excited. A whole day for honest self-evaluation and for planning a better future! For a few years it was very effective. Then I began to find that one day wasn't enough. I found that the problems I was working on required more time. About that time I realized that the "Ten Days of Repentance" from Rosh Hashanah to Yom Kippur should be just what their title says — the effort should not be limited to one day, but spread over ten. That was a big improvement and for a few more years I was content. But then again it seemed that even ten days was not enough to really get a handle on the steps I wanted to take. And then it occurred to me that we start blowing the shofar on Rosh Chodesh Elul (thirty days before the Ten

Days of Repentance). *That's* when I should start my efforts. Since then things have gone very well.

Stories such as these illustrate the personal depth, meaning and idealism that traditional Judaism adds to one's life.

The prevalence of these two motivations for exploring Judaism — the ethnic impulse and the desire for personal growth — is symptomatic of the failures of contemporary education, Jewish and secular. A strong sense of Jewish identity is not provided by non-traditional Jewish education. Rather, the emphasis is on universal humanism, which downplays national and cultural differences. As I have indicated, this approach is false historically. (The detailed argument for this assertion must await another occasion.) In any case, it does nothing for the person who wants to understand his uniqueness as a Jew. No wonder that this type of Jewish education produces assimilation and intermarriage! Furthermore, it creates false impressions about traditional Judaism and Jews, implicitly and/or explicitly.

Consider the question of a Jewish young man in Baltimore who joined Hare Krishna. Observing my (chassidic) dress and my personal commitment to Judaism, he asked: "Is there anyone else like you?" This in *Baltimore*, home of a world-famous yeshivah and a strong traditional community. Or consider the student in Pittsburgh whose class was given an opportunity to question an "Orthodox" woman. He asked about the "tassels" attached to certain garments. She answered, "Those are called *tzitzis*. The Torah says that every four-cornered garment should have them. Nobody wears them anymore." When I was introduced to my rebbe in 1962, the fellow who performed the introduction asked me how many chassidim I thought there were in the United States. "You mean those people in the funny hats and the long black coats? Maybe three." I answered. And I grew up in Westchester County, a mere hour from Brooklyn. How often I meet the expectation that traditional Jews must be uneducated, unsophisticated bumpkins, somehow left over from the Middle Ages. Yet among my religious friends I count members of all the professions — doctors, lawyers, accountants, etc. — including three with Ph.D.s from M.I.T. Misinformation such as this does nothing to give a Jew a sense of his roots.

Equally severe, and far more pervasive, is the failure to address the personal growth of the student. Educational institutions rarely discuss personal goals, character development or practical interpersonal relations. Part of the reluctance to do so stems from the illusion that true democracy requires value-free education. The result is that the values necessary for success in school — intelligence, competitiveness, scholarship, etc. — are rewarded and reinforced. Other values — cooperation, sympathy, self-sacrifice, humility, etc. — are treated as optional or even irrelevant by the school's silence. The effect is particularly tragic on the interpersonal sphere. With 50% of marriages ending in divorce, why are there no classes discussing communication, shared responsibilities, money management and other marital responsibilities? Surely knowing how to repair a damaged friendship, or console someone in pain, is as important as remembering the original thirteen states of America. Now for people who are content with the usual round of work, television, family and community, in that order, with the usual tensions and disappointments, the lack of stimulus and tools for personal growth merely reinforces the limits of their narrow, humdrum lives. But for those who seek to develop noble character, sensitive interpersonal relations, high ideals and a sense of life's significance, personal growth demands attention.

When a Jew is moved by interest in his roots and personal growth to explore Judaism with an open mind, we are challenged to provide sophisticated education and first-hand experience in a sensitive environment. If we meet this challenge, the chances are excellent that he will join the tens of thousands who have committed themselves to their millennial Jewish heritage.